Preface

My friend, Mark Spitsbergen, is a dear brother who loves Jesus with all his heart. He also loves the Scripture and the sound application of truth.

I have been saved since I was 5 years old and baptized in the Holy Spirit since I was 11. I have been preaching the Gospel since I was 15 and in full time ministry since 1989.` I have studied the Bible for 45 years and heard so many angles and perspective and teachings on the subject of grace that I have lost count.

Yet, in this book on grace, Mark brought out something that I never heard from another or discovered in my own studies.

I never connected that grace has inseparably embedded in it the strong sense of gratitude.

My dad was a general contractor and builder, as was his dad, and his dad before him. Our entire family context for generations was the context of construction and the building of complex things.

I grew up working with my dad in his turn-key construction company. We did every trade, and rarely sub-contracted out anything. I was taught most of the trades, and so I continue to think in these terms.

I see this revelation about Grace and Gratitude like the make up of concrete. In general, concrete is made up of 4 basic ingredients: sand, gravel, cement powder, and water. You combine these ingredients in specific proportions and get concrete.

If you leave out the gravel, it is not concrete, but rather mortar used for cementing bricks or blocks together or providing surface coverings, etc. If you leave out the cement powder, all you have is wet sand and gravel.

These different ingredients exist independently of one another and have functions in other ways besides concrete. But you don't look at the piles of sand and gravel, sacks of cement powder, and barrels of water, and call those separate piles of materials "concrete". It's not concrete until they are mixed in the right proportions and given time to set up. Once it sets up, the concrete is cured and has extraordinary uses.

Grace is like this. One of the ingredients that makes up grace, is GRATITUDE. Like concrete, if you take the gratitude out, grace no longer exists. It falls apart into separate piles of power, transformation, generosity, favor, etc.

This stirs my spirit. My wife, Audrey, and I have been anchored by the Father during many years of difficulty, challenges, mistakes, and victories in our life and ministry by giving thanks IN those circumstances. It has insulated us from much stress and trauma.

Without fully understanding the connection of giving thanks and its relation to the activation of God's power in our lives through His Grace, we cultivated the practice of giving thanks and being grateful our entire lives. We tried hard to live Philippians 4:6-7.

Audrey has a "Thank you, Jesus" song that she taught our children. For as long as I have known her, she spontaneously bursts into gratitude about things she sees.

A flower. A sunset. A tree. A mountain. Untampered beauty that God has made prompts gratitude to burst from her heart and through her mouth into praise!

After we had children, she sang her gratitude with them and demonstrated simple and unfatigued joy and thanksgiving as she saw what so many people miss or do not stop to appreciate. She did the same thing with me. Her joy and thanksgiving extended to many aspects of life and became the undertone of the way both of us approach every situation in which we find ourselves. Audrey set the tone of giving thanks in both good and difficult circumstances. Now I realize this released the POWER we experienced in the life struggles we have walked through.

Thanksgiving yields great power to bear the weight of life. The weight of obedience. The weight of resistance.

Now, I better understand why our lifelong propensity for being grateful has served us well.

If part of grace is God's power applied to a believer for transformation, then obedience to the directive in 1 Thessalonians 5:18 to give thanks in all circumstances goes far beyond a proper attitude of the heart. It goes much deeper than merely being a heart posture that positively impacts those in close proximity to you (it is a real drag to be around a cynical, ungrateful person who just complains about everything!).

The teaching of the appropriation of grace in a believer as a discipleship issue can seem daunting, ambiguous, and shrouded in mystery for many disciple makers because of the very real lack of understanding of the grace of God. That's where Dr. Spitsbergen's great work in this book comes in!

What is ringing my bell is that he writes the following about grace: (chairo). Equally, it is used in the sense of benefit and gratitude."

This is amazing and it occurs to me that the command to "give thanks" and the subject of gratitude is an essential mechanism for activating the grace of God in your life.

Intimacy insulates. Gratitude is an expression of love that empowers a greater quality to our intimacy with God and each other. After reading this book, I understand in a deeper way how gratitude is an inseparable nutrient in grace.

Grace is power for transformation, that is, a means by which we walk with God through the Holy Spirit.

I'm meditating on this grace/gratitude connection point and the resulting power we receive IN tough situations as we express our love to God through obedience in giving thanks.

To give thanks is an action we can take to apply the generosity-sense of grace in our life! Any sense of grace active in our life is equal to empowerment. Giving thanks with a genuinely grateful heart is a key to unlock the "power applied" aspect of grace!

Wonder is an essential asset to the ability to be grateful and give thanks!

Contentment factors into our ability to have an attitude of gratitude.

This is so multi-applicable that it could boggle the mind. Consider the following:

As a prisoner for the Lord, then, I urge you to live a life

worthy of the calling you have received. Be completely humble and gentle; be patient, bearing with one another in love. Make every effort to keep the unity of the Spirit through the bond of peace. There is one body and one Spirit, just as you were called to one hope when you were called; one Lord, one faith, one baptism; one God and Father of all, who is over all and through all and in all. Ephesians 4:1-6 NIV

How can we navigate obedience to these verses in times of disagreement with one another? How can we not compromise the truth and at the same time not allow disagreement to destroy the bond of peace that is essential to maintaining unity?

Gratitude unlocks the ability (Grace) in God to walk through (in complete obedience) these paradoxical times with one another.

Giving thanks is something we can do that yields tremendous power for us. It is robustly taught, implied and demonstrated throughout the Bible.

Consider the following:

- In the Bible, 47 books contain at least one verse explicitly mentioning "give thanks," "thanksgiving," or a direct equivalent tied to gratitude.
- 8 books imply gratitude through praise, blessing, or acknowledgment of God's goodness.
- In the Old Testament, 27 books have explicit uses of gratitude and 7 have implied uses (Judges, 1 Kings, 2 Kings, Esther, Ecclesiastes, Ezekiel and Zephaniah).

- In the New Testament, 20 books have explicit uses of gratitude and 1 has implied (James).

Overall Conclusion:

We need to grasp the significance of this gift that is imparted to us in the command to give thanks. It results in a transformed life and enables a connection with God and others that is truly astonishing.

I am not talking about "the power of positive thinking" espoused by some. I am talking about obedience to the command of God that unlocks His power applied in our lives.

His GRACE is His POWER for transformation in us.

You can memorize verses, pray every day, and claim his power, etc., and still have a grumbling and fault-finding attitude. You can claim all you want, but you must also OBEY His words.

God gives us His commands for our benefit. The command to give thanks IN every circumstance (this is completely different from trying to thank God FOR every circumstance), is an essential action of obedience that activates the Grace of God in our lives.

Thank you, Mark, for calling our attention to this vital aspect of God's Grace.

Give thanks in all circumstances and see the Grace of God energize your connection with Him!

Blessings and Life!
—**Britt Hancock**

Grace
The Door is open to All

Pastor Mark Spitsbergen

Grace: The Door is open to All
By Dr. Mark Spitsbergen, ThD, MS
Copyright © 2026 by Abiding Place Ministries, San Diego, CA.

ISBN: 979-8-9944098-3-1

Address correspondence to:

Mark Spitsbergen
Abiding Place Ministries
2155 N Campo Truck Trail, Campo CA 91906
www.AbidingPlace.org
AwakeSD@me.com

All rights reserved.

Table of Contents

Preface ....

Foreward 7

Introduction 11

By Grace We Are Saved...23

Grace Empowers Us 37

Grace Grants Repentance 41

The Blood...51

The Covenant of Blood is a Covenant of Grace Fully Revealed 59

Brief History of the Theology of Grace..........................69

Faith is Our Response to God.......................................73

Salvation For Anyone and Everyone: The Whole World...................83

Jesus Gave the Opportunity to Anyone and Everyone to Be Saved .87

Free Will and The Sovereignty of God..........................95

Repent and Believe 101

Good Works Are Faith Works 105

The Same Grace that Saved Us Matures Us.................111

The Grace that Purchased Us Preserves Us.................115

The Throne of Grace...121

What God Has Willed...129

References...132

Foreward

Grace is the very heartbeat of God's redemptive plan—His unmerited favor, His divine empowerment, and His invitation into fellowship with Him. It is through grace that we are saved, transformed, and sustained in our walk with Him. Grace is not merely a theological concept; it is the very essence of God's love in action.

Dr. Mark Spitsbergen, in this profound and compelling work, unpacks the richness of God's grace as revealed in Scripture. He does not merely define grace but invites us to experience it as the supernatural power of God that redeems, empowers, and sustains every believer. This book is not just an academic exploration; it is an invitation to step into the fullness of Christ, to live in the reality of His grace, and to embrace the life God has made available to us through the covenant of His Son.

From the earliest pages of Scripture to the ultimate revelation of Christ, grace has always been the means by which God interacts with humanity. It is not something earned or deserved but is freely given to all who will receive it. Yet, as Dr. Spitsbergen so effectively illustrates, grace is more than pardon—it is power. Grace does not simply cover sin; it transforms the sinner. It enables us to walk in righteousness, to live in victory, and to fulfill the calling that God has placed on our lives.

In this book, you will discover grace as the means of salvation, the force that grants repentance, the power that enables good works, and the foundation upon which our faith rests. You will be challenged to move beyond a superficial understanding of grace and into the depths of its reality—where grace is not merely a theological stance but a living, active force at work within us.

Dr. Spitsbergen's deep commitment to the authority of Scripture ensures that every insight presented is firmly rooted in God's Word. His exploration of grace is not shaped by theological traditions or human reasoning but by the clear and uncompromising truth of the Bible. This book does not settle for half-measures or partial truths; it boldly declares the fullness of what Christ has accomplished for us and in us.

As you read these pages, may you be awakened to the greatness of God's grace. May you come to know grace not just as a doctrine but as the very power of God working in your life. And may you be inspired to walk in the fullness of all that Christ has provided, living as a testimony to His glory.

This book is more than an exploration of grace—it is a call to live in it.

—Dr Rodney Howard-Browne
President & Founder
Revival Ministries Int (an association of churches) Tampa Florida USA

Introduction

"And of His fullness have all we received, and grace upon grace"

(John 1:16)

The grace of God, which has come to us by Christ Jesus, finds its introduction and sets its precedence as the greatest gift of all. This gift of God goes far beyond any expectation of men – the gift that grace has brought is the gift of the fullness of Christ Jesus. Christ Jesus came to save sinners. It does not matter how desperately wicked a person has been, God invites us into the family. God is at work to save every person to the uttermost that comes to Him by Jesus Christ[1]. His gift of grace invites us to receive all the life that He possesses[2].

Osborne writes concerning His fullness that we have received,

> "'Out of his fullness,' showing that God's people ('we all') have 'received' the benefits of his fullness in the salvation gifts that come from God. The Word has

---

[1] (Heb. 7:25)
[2] (John 1:16, Eph. 4:13, Col. 1:19, 2:9, 10)

filled us with his divine blessings, the greatest of which is himself"

(Grant Osborne, 2018)

"The fullness of the Godhead dwelleth in Him and out of this fullness we receive grace upon grace, and that we might also be filled with all the fullness of God (Eph. 3:19)"

(Arno C. Gaebelein, 2009)

The grace of God has brought to us every dimension of salvation that is expressed in the Bible. The grace of God has granted to us a fellowship without limitation[3]. God made a way for us to be one with Himself through His only begotten Son. Christ Jesus supplied the sacrifice of Himself so that we may exist in Him, and He in us. We find that in every dimension of grace – God is doing for us what we could never do for ourselves. Grace teaches us everything that pleases God and also empowers us to do all that our heavenly Father desires. We begin as newborn babies and grow and mature in Him as we simply say, "Yes," to all He has done and yield to what only He can do for us[4]. We have received His divine nature and everything that pertains to His life and godliness so that we may inherit the glorious and abundant life of Christ Jesus[5].

---

[3] (John 6:56, 14:21, 17:21-22, 1 John 3:24, 4:15, 16, 4:12, 13)
[4] (1 Pet. 2:2; 1 John 2:12; 1 Cor. 3:1; 1 Tim. 4:6)
[5] (2 Peter 1:3-4; John 10:10)

"The grace then that is with us is not like theirs (those of the Old Covenant). For not only was pardon of sins given to us, (since this we have in common with them, for all have sinned) but righteousness also, and sanctification, and sonship, and the gift of the Spirit far more glorious and more abundant"

(Chrysostom 1884).

All men are spiritually lost, living in spiritual darkness, but God has caused His light to shine upon us. Those lost in sin are blinded by the god of this world, yet God has supplied deliverance for all who are willing[6]. God in His great grace stepped in and has changed the heart of everyone who will believe and has brought us into His kingdom. God has given us a new heart and a new spirit so that we may be able to understand His ways. He has put His Holy Spirit in us so that we can be taught of God. He has given us the ability to learn who He is and what He has purposed for our lives. The training that only God the Holy Spirit can give is ours so that we can develop in all the ways of His likeness[7]. We do not have to rely on our own ability to do what pleases God. We simply agree with Him and He becomes our strength and defense. Christ Jesus is the One Who overcame sin and all the powers of darkness and now He, Who is greater than the one who is

---
[6] (Acts 26:18)
[7] (Rom 8:29; 2 Cor 3:18)

in the world, dwells in us. Because the overcomer lives within, we learn to overcome as He overcame[8]. God has given us all things that pertain to His life and godliness[9]. In this great grace He allows us to share in His glory and honor – a glory and honor that we could never deserve. He bought and paid for us, rescuing us from the slavery sin and has a love for us that lasts forever. His grace has given us the ability to also love Him as He has loved us[10]. If we sin, He is there to intercede on our behalf, and in love and mercy He shows us how to live the majestic and eternal life of God. Through His great grace, sin does not have the same consequence that it had with Adam. Adam had to wait for a coming Redeemer to deal with his trespass and sin, but for us our Redeemer is here! All we have to do is call and He answers and empowers us with the ability to walk with Him.

Grace can only be defined by the Scripture, and in the Scripture alone. Integrating the Scripture with philosophical ideas and personal experience will never result in what God's Word alone will produce. We are to understand the Scripture by the Scripture, not by extra-biblical sources. Augustine, the Reformers, the Canons of Dort, or the Arminians do not have the right to give us non-biblical definitions of grace that we must then choose from if we are to have correct doctrine. Only the Scripture

---

[8] (1 John 4:3,13; Rom. 8:31;1 John 2:13,27; Rev. 3:21)
[9] (2 Pet. 1:3)
[10] (Rom 5:5)

can properly define the manifold grace of God and its true meaning.

Theology thinks of salvation in terms of it being either positional or relational. The theological idea of these terms is that if it is positional, our standing before God is unchanging no matter what we do. Whereas relational Christianity understands salvation as the privilege to enter into a loving relationship with God wherein we are trained and developed in His ways. Christ Jesus is absolutely the Lord our righteousness and we find all of our life in Him. Yet, what is even more underscored in the New Testament is that He is in us.

There are also different positions as to whether righteousness is imputed or imparted. The concept of imputed righteousness is that God credits Jesus' righteousness to each person, while imparted righteousness is God enabling us to live the life that pleases Him by dwelling in us. Certainly both imputed righteousness and imparted righteousness are meaningful to our life in Christ Jesus. However, what is perfectly clear in scripture is that Christ Jesus dwells in us[11]. Christ Jesus is all our righteousness, and it's His life imparted to us that imparts His righteousness[12]. He has imputed His righteousness to us in a similar way as it was imputed to Abraham. God imputed righteousness to Abraham

---

[11] (Col. 1:27; John 14:17; 1 John 3:24; John 6:56)
[12] (1 Cor. 1:30; 2 Cor. 5:21; Phil. 3:9; Rom. 4:24-25; Jer. 23:6; 33:16)

because he believed – he believed in the coming Seed, his Redeemer Christ Jesus[13]. We now possess more than what Abraham had, for now we are made the righteousness of God in Him[14]. It's His righteousness not only imputed but imparted, for Christ Jesus dwells within us[15]. We know that we have been made the righteousness of God because Christ Jesus is in us by the Spirit Who He has given us – this is an unquestionable righteousness. He has imparted His life, which is His imparted righteousness[16]. This is a righteousness that Paul defines when, after discussing imputed righteousness, he takes up the topic of imparted righteousness in Rom 6:1-8:39.

> "His thanksgiving fits within his emphasis on sanctification, the impartation of righteousness in 6:1—8:39"
>
> (James E. Rosscup, 1998)

The idea that God's salvation results in only a "positional righteousness" infringes on the power of change through the miracle of the new creation. It also challenges individual responsibility and accountability for sin. The basis for the theory of "positional righteousness" is that we are not really free from the sin nature and will go on sinning. As sinners then, God provided a means by

---

[13] (Gal. 3:15; John 8:56; Gen. 22:8)
[14] (2 Cor 5:21)
[15] (Col. 1:27; 1 John 3:24 etc...)
[16] (Gal. 3:21)

which our position before God does not change regardless of our sin. This makes the result of God's grace only a partial salvation, leaving the redeemed, to some degree, in bondage to sin. This does not square with the first great definition of grace revealed in the New Covenant – "and of His fullness have all we received" (John 1:16). The change is radical because it's described in terms of a miraculous new birth[17]. As long as we believe that sin still has power over us, how can we be less than slaves to its power? God has said it shall have no more dominion over us and has instead given us the dominion[18]. The One who is greater than the one who is in the world dwells in us! The dominion and authority of Christ in us is the faith that we now have. Christ in us is the nature of God in our lives. The Holy Spirit dwelling in us produces the fruits of the Spirit in all goodness and righteousness and truth[19].

> "There is no spiritual force in the universe that can overpower the forces of God within us"
>
> (Case & Holdren, 2006)

Understanding all that God has revealed about what Jesus Christ has done for us is challenging. The Bible certainly puts forth a great salvation that has accomplished great things for us that surpass all that we could ever think or ask. Many of those things which God

---

[17] (John 3:3-6; Eph. 4:24; Col. 3:10: 2 Cor. 5:17 etc…)
[18] (Rom. 6:14-17, 8:2; 1 Jn. 4:4; 5:18)
[19] (Ephesians 5:9; Gal. 5:22; Rom. 14:17; John 4:14; 7:38-39)

has done for us seem so beyond the possibility of our present life. As a result, many who are critical of "this so great salvation" speak of it in terms of "now but not yet." They cannot deny that the great things that God has revealed in His Word, and that He has done for us, and what we are empowered to do are scriptural. So they are said to be, "Things that are ours now, but will not be realized until we get to Heaven." However, this is not the case. All of these blessings and promises that we find in the New Testament are ours right now – this is the covenant. All of God's promises are truly "Yes and amen" (2 Cor. 1:20).

We should not seek to explain away what God says in His Word, but rather simply embrace it. If we do not agree with the report of the Lord, then the miracle power of His Word will not be realized in our lives[20]. It is by believing the Word of God that faith comes, and faith then produces the miracles. Our responsibility is to simply believe what God has said. If we will believe what God has said, then we will have the miracle that only faith can produce. This is especially true about grace. The subject of grace is about all that God has done for us. Scripture cannot be bent to serve the ideas and interest of those who hold to a determinist concept that every action of our life has been predetermined. Determinists deny the freedom of choice and as a result full responsibility for their choices. Neither

---

[20] (Rom. 10:16-17; 1 Thess. 2:13; Gal. 3:2)

can the meaning of grace be understood in terms of having earned it or deserved it on the basis of a person's behavior. Grace is all about what God has done for us and what only God can continue to do in us.

Wherever God is at work, His grace is revealed. Whenever He interacted with men, He always displayed His grace. God's grace is displayed in both the Old and New Testament. God's grace was there when Eve was deceived. He looked in her eyes, now darkened by her sin, and promised her the coming Seed. When Cain killed his brother and refused to repent in his self-pity, God promised to protect him so that he would not be killed. Men had become so wicked that God repented that He made them, yet still in His grace He was willing to intervene and start over with man. His grace was then displayed in Noah and His family who prepared the ark that God had revealed to protect and keep them from His wrath.

God's grace is expressed by Hebrew words like חֵן ('chen'), and its many derivatives like חַנּוּן ('channun'). The Hebrew word 'channun' has a special place in the description of grace. Keeping in mind that God is unchanging. He is the same today as He was in the eternal past. God was not a different person in the Old Testament than He is in the New Testament. The Hebrew word channun is one of the words that God used to fully reveal Himself to Moses. God said,

> *"Yehovah, Yehovah, God, Who is compassionate and gracious, slow to anger, and abounding with lovingkindness and faithfulness"*
>
> -Exodus 34:6

This was the full revelation of who God is in the Old Testament. That revelation is now fully revealed in a greater way through Christ Jesus, who is the full expression of His glory and revelation of His person[21].

The primary Hebrew word for grace, חֵן ('chen')., is found 70 times in the Old Testament. In all, there are six important words derived from the root: חָנַן 'chānan'; חֵן 'chēn'; חַנּוּן 'channûn'; חֲנִינָה 'chanînâ'; תְּחִנָּה 'techinnâ'; תַּחֲנוּן 'tachanûn.' "The noun is first a term of beauty, and secondly, favor. In the Old Testament, it is used to give favor and also to show favor. It has two basic meanings: favor and grace. With rare exceptions, God is the One Who is said to give favor. The first occurance of 'chen' in the Old Testament is in Genesis 6:8, in which Noah, being righteous and a perfect man in contrast to the wicked of His generation, found "grace in the eyes of the Lord." Keeping in mind that no matter how perfect a man is, He is still in need of the righteousness that only God can give.

The Greek word used to translate חֵן ('chen') in the Septuagint (LXX) is 'cháris.' 'Cháris' is the word used in the New Testament for grace. The Greek word 'cháris' is

---

[21] (Heb. 1:3; Col. 1:19; 2:9; John 14:9; Mt. 11:27; Ex. 33:22)

found 156 times in the Majority Text of the New Testament. Like its Hebrew equivalent, it is primarily translated as "grace" or "favor." In classical Greek, the word finds its expression in joy, generosity, and love, which is also the meaning of its root word χαιρω ('chairo'). Equally, it is used in the sense of benefit and gratitude. The first occurance of grace found in the four Gospels was the angel's address to Mary in which she was called highly favored and the one who found "favor with God" (Luke 1:30). Yet, most importantly, Jesus Christ, the only begotten Son of God, Who is the Word made flesh, is the One Who fully reveals the meaning of grace.

With a combined 226 verses in which both the Hebrew or Greek word for grace is found, we have more than enough information to properly understand and define the meaning of grace from the Scriptures. What is most important though is defining the meaning of the word in the context of the nature and character of God. In the revelation of Himself, He showed that His mercy, love, longsuffering and truth are inseparable from His grace.

When God says be holy just as He is holy, we know His grace has empowered us to have the majestic life that He has. He asks us to be holy and He supplies the ability, we simply respond to Him with our will. He tells us to be conformed to the image of the Son and by His grace He empowers us with all that we need by the Holy Spirit to do it. He tells us to walk as He walks, to imitate God, to be as

He is in this world, to love like He loves – and once again, the grace of God that brought us His salvation enables us to do so[22]. To see Him, to know Him, to have our eyes opened to the wonders of His love and the riches of His glory, leaves us in a place of awe and wonder at the honor and privilege of being His.

---

[22] (Titus 2:11-12)

By Grace We Are Saved

We cannot find a more revealing statement about the powerlessness of the Law and the life-giving power of the New Covenant than this:

> "Is the Law then against the promises of God? God forbid – for if there had been a law which could have **given life**, truly righteousness should have been by the Law."
>
> (Gal. 3:21)

When God imparted His life into us, He imparted His righteousness. He came into our lives and flooded our souls with His life and goodness. This wonderful life brought a new kind of law, the law of the Spirit of life that is in Christ Jesus. The life of the Spirit made us free from the law of sin and death[23]. The Law of Moses left everyone under the bondage of sin and death. The law of the Spirit of Life imparted the life of God and liberated us from the bondage of sin and death. The life of God imparted resulted in the righteousness of God imparted[24]. Grace came to us by Jesus Christ, Who raised us up from

---

[23] (Rom. 8:2; John 3:6)
[24] (Rom. 3:22, 8:1-4, 10:3, 2 Cor. 5:17, 21)

spiritual death by the new birth and imparted the life giving Spirit of God[25].

> "If the law had been capable of giving life, "verily (in very reality, and not in the mere fancy of legalists) righteousness would have been by the law (for where life is, there is righteousness…)"
>
> (Jamieson, Fausset and Brown, 1997).

The New Covenant is established in the life-giving blood of Jesus[26], which is referred to as the blood of the everlasting covenant[27]. The blood released us from our sins when we first repented of them and were born again. The blood washes us from our sins, even if we should commit those sins again[28]. The blood was shed for our sins, and not for ours only but for the whole world[29]. Therefore, it is the blood of God that has established the Covenant of Grace. All of the benefits of the New Covenant must be comprehended in what the blood of Jesus has accomplished – not just righteousness and holiness, but every dimension of the life of God. When we define grace, we must then define it on the basis of all that God has done for us in Christ Jesus, beginning with the

---

[25] (Rom. 6:4, 8:2,10; Eph. 2:5)
[26] (Luke 22:20)
[27] (Heb. 13:20)
[28] (1 John 1:9)
[29] (1 John 2:2)

new birth, but including the future resurrected glorified body.

By grace we are saved (Eph. 2:8). Therefore, when we define what it means to be saved, we also define what grace has done. Paul defines salvation on the basis of being washed with the water of regeneration and renewing of the Holy Spirit[30]. Therefore, grace is the means by which we are born again: born of the Spirit and of the water. Grace would then also be defined as the means by which we received a new heart and a new spirit, along with the very Spirit of God placed inside of us[31]. Grace has caused us to be recreated in Christ Jesus[32] – old things have passed away, and behold all things are new[33]! It is grace that brought forth the divine nature in our lives through being born of the Spirit[34]. By the grace that God has supplied as to newborn babies, we continue to grow up into all of that which Christ Jesus has done for us[35].

Our doctrines of grace and of faith should be built on the new creation and the divine nature that the miracle of grace has brought to us[36]. There is a miraculous change that has been brought to us by grace. If we deny the change that has taken place in our lives, then our

---

[30] (Titus 3:5)
[31] (Ezekiel 36:26)
[32] (Eph. 4:23-24)
[33] (2 Cor. 5:17)
[34] (2 Pet. 1:4; John 3:5; Rom 8:9)
[35] (Eph. 4:15; 2 Peter 3:18)
[36] (2 Cor. 5:17; 2 Peter 1:3-4; Eph. 4:24)

doctrines will reflect that. We cannot have a salvation that leaves us unchanged and in some measure slaves to Satan and his sin. We cannot leave righteousness in an imputed realm, when it has also been imparted. We cannot make our relationship with God purely "positional" or "legal," when God has placed responsibility on us for our actions. The life in Christ Jesus is a walk and a life together with Him[37].

Being born again includes being spiritually recreated after God's image in righteousness and true holiness[38]. Grace supplies us with everything that the Holy Spirit has come to do for us and through us. He is the One Who leads us and guides us into all the truth[39]. He is the One Who teaches us all things[40] and reveals all that Christ Jesus has done for us and is doing for us now[41]. The Holy Spirit, Who we received, is the very Spirit of Holiness and Fountainhead from which the righteousness of God flows[42]. He is the One Who glorifies Jesus and brings all that Christ Jesus has done and is doing into our lives[43]. He keeps us, upholds us, perfects us, empowers us, convicts us, delivers us, secures us, intercedes for us, reveals Jesus

---

[37] (Heb 11:5-6; Rom 8:1,4; Gal 5:16,25; Phil 3:20)
[38] (Eph. 4:24; Col. 3:10)
[39] (John 16:13, 14:17, 15:26)
[40] (John 14:26)
[41] (John 16:13-14, 1 Cor. 2:10-11)
[42] (Jn 4:14; 7:38-39)
[43] (John 16:13-15)

to us, and protects us. The Holy Spirit is the Spirit of Grace[44].

We have no authority to limit the attributes of the life of Christ Jesus that we have been given. Paul's prayer concerning the grace of God that is brought to us by Christ Jesus is that He would count us worthy of the calling, and fulfill all of the good pleasure of His goodness, with the work of faith and power, so that the name of our Lord Jesus Christ would be glorified in us, and we in Him[45]. His prayer was that we would have our eyes opened to understand the inheritance that God has in us, and the exceeding greatness of His power that was given to us[46]. Grace upon grace has blessed us with not only being born of the Spirit but also baptized in the Spirit of Holiness. The Holy Spirit is in us and flows out of us like rivers. God has overwhelmed us with His presence and has come to dwell in the midst of our lives. In the days of Moses God desired to dwell in their midst, but they failed to properly respond to His desire. Yet still because of His mercy and grace was willing to remain but had to live outside their camp[47].

The testimony of all the writers of the New Testament, and the testimony of Jesus, was that the Holy Spirit would be with us and in us, and He would empower us to do the

---

[44] (Heb. 10:29; Titus 2:11; Eph 4:30)
[45] (2 Thess. 1:11-12)
[46] (Eph. 1:17-19)
[47] (Ex. 25:8, 33:7)

works of Jesus. He would dwell in us and teach us, mentoring every dimension of our lives. He would be the gift and the supply of all those things provided for us as a new creation[48].

All of the nature of God is expressed through our lives by the Holy Spirit, which Paul referred to as the fruits of the Spirit. However, that is not the only outworking of the Holy Spirit, for God has also supplied the gifts of the Spirit. He has given us the ability by the Holy Spirit to walk in signs and wonders and the demonstration of the power of the Holy Spirit; it was this kind of inworking of the Holy Spirit that Paul called the full gospel[49]. God has supplied the inworking of the Holy Spirit so that the outworking of His power and ability would be like a wellspring in our souls. To deny the outworking or works of the Spirit is to deny His fruits as well as His power in our lives. Jesus so emphasized the outworking of the Holy Spirit manifested through our lives that He went beyond just a wellspring and described the outworking of the Holy Spirit like rivers! The rivers of God's life flowing into us by the Holy Spirit and flowing out by the Holy Spirit to give witness that Jesus is the Son of God and was raised from the dead[50]. These are the things that Jesus and His Apostles emphasized in describing the grace that came by

---

[48] (John 14:16, 7:38-39, 14:17-23; 2 Tim. 1:14; Rom. 14:17; 2 Cor. 6:6; 1 Peter 1:2, 12, 22; Jude 1:20 etc.)
[49] (Rom. 15:19; 1 Cor. 2:4-5; 1 Thess. 1:5)
[50] (John 7:39, Acts 2:33)

Jesus Christ. To fail to include the outworking of the Holy Spirit through our lives in the definition of grace is more than a shortcoming.

For by grace we are saved through faith (Eph. 2:8). Once again, the faith of the New Testament is defined by the new creation. The new creation is what the New Covenant is all about. The promised Seed has come and recreated us anew in Christ Jesus. The new creation is what was prophesied by the prophets when they described the New Covenant that God would make. The new creation is the context of the entire New Testament. We understand all that Paul described of the righteousness of God in the context of being born again. Righteousness by faith is the faith of Jesus Christ that resulted in us being born again. Paul's description of the faith of the New Covenant is the same description that Jesus gave when He said: you must be born again[51]. This is the shocking and glorious reality of the New Covenant.

The New Covenant is not the form and ritual of the Law, confined in an unregenerate state of the flesh. It's not circumcision or uncircumcision, but a new creation[52]. The new creation is that which is born of the Spirit to now live in the Spirit[53]. It's the transition from the unregenerate state of flesh to the regenerated state of the Spirit. It's no longer of the human ability, but of the ability which only

---

[51] (John 3:3-6; 2 Cor. 5:17-18)
[52] (Gal. 6:15)
[53] (Rom. 8:1-9)

God can give[54]. The faith of the New Testament is Christ Jesus in us – this is the display of God's grace[55]. To make the faith of the New Testament something less than being made a new creation is altogether missing the point.

Why focus on one single part of the life of God when we have the fullness of Jesus? Once again, Grace is defined in the miracle of receiving all of God's fullness[56]. We have received His Spirit, His life, His righteousness, His holiness, His purity, His glory, and His divine nature. The disastrous and sinful effect of Adam's transgression was done away with, just as the Law was done away with through the obedience of Christ Jesus. Adam brought the dominion of sin into our lives, the Law revealed that sin, but Christ Jesus destroyed both in His own body. Christ Jesus bore our sins in His own body so that we could be dead to sin and alive to righteousness, Hallelujah[57]. He has written His laws on the table of our hearts so that our very nature agrees with God[58]. The grace that brought salvation created a new man. The former life of Adam was destroyed through the body of His flesh. The life of God was imparted by the Spirit through the blood of the everlasting covenant.

---

[54] (Gal. 4:21-31)
[55] (Col. 1:27)
[56] (John 1:16; Col. 2:9-10)
[57] (1 Pet. 2:24)
[58] (Heb. 8:10, 10:16; 2 Cor. 3:3)

"Christ is the personal and bodily manifestation of all the fullness of Deity. He was God incarnate and the manifestation of all the fullness of God's power and blessings to men (Isa. 7:14; 9:6; Mt. 1:18–25; Lk. 1:34–35)"

(Dake, 1997).

Once again, when Christ Jesus came into our lives, we cannot say that just some part of His life came in – all of His life came in. We are now supposed to live by Him[59]. When we were made the temple of the Holy Ghost, the Lord placed His dwelling place within our lives[60]. As His temple our inner man is His Holy of Holies, for God dwells there[61]. He now dwells in us with all His fullness! This is grace. This is the faith of the New Testament. This is the work of grace that brought to us this unspeakable gift, which includes the whole of His life: His righteousness and holiness.

For by grace we were saved, and that not of ourselves (Eph. 2:8). There was nothing that any man could ever do to deliver himself from the bondage of sin and death. Even the covenant of the Law was powerless to deliver men from the bondage of sin and death. The Covenant of the Law was powerless to impart the life of God, therefore the righteousness of God that comes forth from the life of

---

[59] (Gal. 2:20)
[60] (Heb. 9:8)
[61] (1 Cor. 3:16; 2 Cor. 6:16)

God could not come by the Covenant of the Law. How did it come? It came by the shed blood of Jesus Christ. Through the death of Jesus, He destroyed the power of Satan over our lives. Through the obedience of Christ the consequence of the disobedience of Adam was destroyed and broken off of our lives. Through the obedience of Christ Jesus many were made righteous, as many as would believe[62]. Through this great grace of God, we do those things that are contained in the Law by nature (Rom. 8:4). We were made holy by what He did on the cross, when He was made a curse for us. Through His resurrection we received the inward resurrection and became the house in which God dwells[63].

> "We must have a new bias; 'a new heart must be given us, and a new spirit be put within us,' if we would persevere unto the end. Let us not then expect to prevail by legal considerations, or legal endeavors. Let us indeed condemn sin in the purpose of our minds, and sentence it to death: but let us look to Christ for strength, and maintain the conflict in dependence on his power and grace. Then, though unable to do any thing of ourselves, we shall be enabled to 'do all things'"
>
> (Charles Simeon, 1833).

---

[62] (Rom. 5-12-21, John 1:12)
[63] (Col. 3:1, 2:12; Rom. 6:4; 2 Cor. 6:16)

For by grace we were saved, and that not of ourselves, it is the gift of God (Eph 2:8). The righteousness and the true holiness that we now have in Christ Jesus came from Christ Jesus as a gift. It can not be earned and it could never be deserved! It's His righteousness, not the righteousness of men. It's His holiness, not the holiness of men. He gave us the righteousness of God. He also gave us the holiness of God. How? He gave us His life. We were born of Him[64]. We were given the authority to be the sons of God[65]. This is the context of grace.

> "Because you are His sons, God sent the Spirit of his Son into our hearts, crying, 'God's my Father!'"
>
> (Gal. 4:6).

After He rose from the dead, Jesus sent a message to His brethren,

> "I am ascending to My Father, and your Father, to My God and your God"
>
> (John 20:17).

Now that we have His righteousness, we can be righteous just as He is righteous[66], Now that we have received His Holiness, we can be holy just as He is Holy[67].

---

[64] (John 1:13)
[65] (John 1:12)
[66] (1 John 2:29; 3:7)
[67] (Mt. 5:48, Luke 1:75; 1 Pet. 1:15-17; 2 Peter 3:11)

The Apostle Paul certainly made an emphasis on righteousness by faith, which is supplied by the grace of God. The emphasis was made in the context of the Jews who claimed righteousness by the Law. Righteousness by the Law is defined by those who go about to establish their own righteousness[68]. There are few in the modern western world that would claim righteousness by the Law. We certainly do not know of anyone outside of the various sects of Judaism that are keeping the Law to obtain a status of righteousness. The Apostle Paul talked more about works than anyone else. Many today fail to recognize how much instruction and admonishment that the Apostle Paul gave on faith works. Many make a fundamental mistake of grouping all works in the category of "Law works." However, the deeds of our lives will either show that we are the living epistle of Christ Jesus or something else[69].

> "Grace is given not because we have done good works but in order that we may have power to do them, not because we have fulfilled the law but in order that we may be able to fulfill it."
>
> -Augustine (Gerald Bray, 1998)

"Now what does he mean by 'grace'? That word is a kind of shorthand for the whole sum of the

---

[68] (Rom 10:3)
[69] (2 Cor 3:3; Heb 8:10, 10:16; Mt 7:16; James 3:11)

unmerited blessings which come to men through Jesus Christ."

(Alexander MacLaren, 2009)

Grace Empowers Us

Grace empowers us with a divine ability that only belongs to God. This special divine empowerment that demonstrated the power that only God possesses is not limited to the New Testament. It was observed in Moses, Joshua, the deliverers of Judges, Samuel, David, priests, prophets, and kings. These were divine abilities granted to them by the Spirit of the Lord. The grace of God was also observed when the word of the Lord came to Zerubbabel. He was told it's not by might nor by power but by my Spirit says the Lord. The mountain of hindrance that was before him was to be made a plain by the shoutings of "Grace! Grace!" (Zech. 4:6-7)

The grace that was given to Moses was a divine ability that was such a part of His life that he was able to take some of the glory that was in his life and impart it to 70 others[70]. The power of Jesus was observed in the lives of the disciples, which was similarly granted to them by Jesus. Later, we observe that the disciples were able to give witness to the resurrection of Jesus with a great display of power because of the great grace that was upon them[71].

---

[70] (Num. 27:20)
[71] (Acts 4:33)

The measure of the gifts of the Spirit that a person has differs on the basis of the grace that is given[72]. Paul himself ministered both the revelation of the Word and the authority of the Word based upon the grace that was given to him[73]. It is important to note that this was a grace that Paul said He received for obedience to the faith[74]. Paul further refined this by saying that it was by the grace of God that He was able to labor more than all of the other apostles. It's understood that grace may be defined in different ways based on the action of God, but it's still grace. For example: prevenient grace, efficacious grace, regenerating grace, sanctifying grace, renovating grace, gifting grace, enabling grace, discomfiting grace, preserving grace, dying grace, glorifying grace and in as many different ways as grace has been demonstrated. What is common to every expression of grace whether it's in the Old or New Testament: is grace is God's divine empowerment given to men to do those things which only He can do. Grace is given to us so that God's will can be fulfilled in our lives.

These things concerning grace were witnessed by Paul who credited grace as the active power that was in him, enabling him to do all that he did[75]. Obviously, Paul is referring to more than just preaching the Word, because

---

[72] (Rom. 12:6)
[73] (Rom. 12:3, 1 Cor. 3:10)
[74] (Rom. 1:5, 15:15)
[75] (1 Cor. 15:10)

we know he ministered with mighty signs and wonders and demonstration of the Holy Spirit when he preached[76]. Of course, Paul is using his life as an example. If Paul's ministry was done with the ability imparted by grace for him, then it must be so for all God's people, both then and now. Grace is the divine favor of God that gives us the ability to do the things that only God can do. It's His power at work in us that allows us to understand every dimension of the love of Christ Jesus[77]. God is at work in us! Grace is the excellency of His power at work in earthen vessels, It's Christ in us, it's according to His power that now resides on the inside of us[78]. Without Christ Jesus we can do nothing but by Him and through Him we can do all things through Christ who strengthens us[79].

Paul makes a unique distinction when he refers to not just grace, but all grace that God would abundantly supply so that we could always have all sufficiency in all things[80]. Paul showed that all blessings and abilities sprang forth from the grace of God. He credited everything He was able to do and accomplish to God's divine ability at work in his life.

---

[76] (Rom. 15:19)
[77] (Eph. 3:18-20)
[78] (Php. 2:13; Eph. 1:19; 3:7, 20; 2 Cor. 3:5; 4:7; Col. 1:29; Mt. 10:20)
[79] (John 14:5; Phil 4:13)
[80] (2 Cor. 9:8)

"but I labored more abundantly than them all: yet not I, but the grace of God which was with me"
                                            (1 Cor. 15:10c).

Grace Grants Repentance

The opportunity that is given to all men to repent is brought to us by the grace of God. Paul said very specifically that, "The grace of God that brings salvation has appeared to all men, teaching us to deny ungodliness and worldly lust..." God has granted to everyone the ability of "repentance unto life." There are primarily two words that are used for repentance in the New Testament: μετανοέω ('metanoeo') and μεταμέλομαι ('metamelomai'). 'Metanoeo' is used for repentance more than the other, 38 times. The basic meaning of 'metanoeo' is "to change the mind," but it also implies a complete reversal of a person's actions as well as their lives. The Hebrew equivalent of 'metanoeo' is נחם, ('nacham'). The Hebrew word 'nachum' is primarily used of God repenting and is translated by 'metanoeo' in the LXX[81]. It is also used with regards to men repenting[82]. Finally, 'metanoeo' is translated several times by the Hebrew word שוב ('shuv') which means to return[83]. In view of this we can be certain that repent and

---

[81] (Amos 7:3,6; Joel 2:13,14; Jonah 3:9,10; 4:2; Zech 8:14; Jer 4:28; 18:8,10)
[82] (Jer 8:6; 38:19)
[83] (Isa 46:8)

repentance is a word that is used for more than the initial salvation experience.

The message of repentance is central to the preaching of the gospel and the work of grace that has granted us "repentance unto life." Repentance is a divine act that takes place because of the working of the Holy Spirit that brings conviction and the blood of Jesus that then cleanses when a person seeks forgiveness of sins[84]. Every person begins a new life in Christ Jesus through the act of repentance which would then result in being born again. Yet, the opportunity to be forgiven for any act of transgression against God after being born again is also granted to each person. We are promised by God that He will forgive us as many times as we need as long as we are also willing to forgive,

> *"Then Peter came to him, and said, Lord, how often shall my brother sin against me, and I forgive him? till seven times? Jesus said to him, I say not unto you, Until seven times: but, Until seventy times seven."*
> *"So likewise shall my heavenly Father do also unto you, if you from your hearts forgive not every one his brother their trespasses."*
> (Mt 18:21–22, 35)

---

[84] (Acts 5:31; 11:18; 13:38; 26:18; Eph 1:7; Col 1:14; James 5:15)

The message of repentance was the introductory theme of Jesus' ministry[85]. It also remains as a banner theme for the preaching of the Gospel to this day[86].

Repentance and faith toward God has been supplied to us and empowers us to live the life of God. However, the grace of God extends beyond just the change of life through the new creation. The grace of God supplies all forgiveness of sins, **if** we sin[87]. Of course, there are many examples of this in Scripture, but a few are addressed by Paul. Paul dealt with the need for repentance and forgiveness of sins in the church at Corinth,

> *"For godly sorrow works repentance to salvation not to be repented of, but the sorrow of the world works death."*
>
> (2 Cor. 7:10)

He also further describes the grace of God that urges men to repent of their sins in 2 Cor. 12:21,

> *"Unless, when I come again, my God will humble me among you, that I shall bewail many who have sinned already, and have **not repented** of the uncleanness and fornication and lasciviousness that they have committed."*

---

[85] (Mt. 4:17; 9:13)
[86] (Luke 24:27)
[87] (1 Jn. 1:9, 2:1; 2 Cor 7:10; James 5:15-16; Eph 4:32; Mt 26:75; Luke 22:32; Mt 6:12; Lk 6:37, 11:4, etc.)

Jesus also addressed the churches in the Book of Revelation and admonished them to repent. In fact, the word for repentance is found more in the book of Revelation than any single book of the New Testament.

There is a lexical synonym for repent in Acts 3:19 which is ἐπιστρέφω ('epistrepho'), which means "to turn",

> *"Repent ('metanoeo') therefore, and turn ('epistrepho'), that your sins may be blotted out, when the times of refreshing come from the presence of the Lord."*
>
> (Acts 3:27)

The same word is used again as an expression of repentance in Acts 28:27[88], which is also a quote from Isa. 6:10. saying,

> *"Go to this people and say, 'With your ears shall you hear, and shall not understand; and with your eyes shall you see, and not perceive. For the heart of this people has grown fat, and their ears are hard of hearing, and their eyes have they closed, lest they should see with their eyes, and hear with their ears, and understand with their hearts, and should turn ('epistrepho'), and I should heal them'"*
>
> (Acts 28:26-27).

---

[88] (*cr* Mk. 4:12)

Through the grace of God that brings salvation, the sins of the past were dealt with through faith in the blood of Jesus that brought the washing of the water of regeneration[89]. Our sins were removed as far as the East is from the West, to be remembered no more[90]. Our sins of the past have been completely blotted out and there should be no more remembrance of them[91]. However, for sins that are committed after we have been made a new creation, we have a High Priest, Christ Jesus, Who is the Intercessor for our sins. This intercession is described in terms of the Old Testament Yom Kippur (the day of cleansing) twice by John[92]. Christ Jesus has become the 'hilasmos' or the 'kaporit' (Hebrew equivalent) for our sins. Also sharing the same root and the same basic meaning is ἱλαστήριον ('hilasteron'), which is used by Paul in Rom. 3:23 and Heb. 9:5. Christ Jesus is the mercy seat. The mercy seat was the place where God met with man and any sins that were committed that affected the Holy of Holies were purified from off the altar[93]. Yet, during the course of the year anyone who sinned was also required to bring a representative offering for a cleansing for their sins[94].

---

[89] (Rom. 3:25, Titus 3:5)
[90] (Heb 8:12; 10:17; Ps 103:12)
[91] (Jer. 31:34, Acts 3:19, Heb. 8:12)
[92] (1 John 2:2, 4:10)
[93] (Ex 30:10; Lev 16:16)
[94] (Lev 4:7,9, 22-25, 30 etc.)

The mercy seat in the Covenant of the Law was the place of intercession where the sins that Israel committed were atoned/ wiped away. Their sins had resulted in the absence of God's presence from the Holy of Holies. When the priest made intercession, the sins of Israel were wiped away – the sins that Israel had committed for the past year were removed from the presence of God. Through the intercession of the blood, which represented the blood of Jesus, the presence of God was invited back in. So, in a similar way, the blood of Jesus cleanses us from our sins. However, as is the type, even so is the antitype. There has to be a confession of those sins and a turning from them or sending them away as represented by the goat for Azazel (scape goat) which was sent away[95]. However, the type does not end there. Everyone's individual sin had to be answered with a sacrifice for sin, confession of the sin and the application of the blood[96]. The difference is that Jesus has offered His blood once for all. The blood remains forever efficacious to forgive sin. If we confess our sins, He is faithful and righteous to cleanse us from all sin and make intercession as our Great High Priest[97]. He is the Lamb of God and it is His blood that has been supplied for the cleansing of sin[98].

---

[95] (Leviticus 16:10)
[96] (Lev. 3:2,8,13; 4:3-7,24,33, etc)
[97] (1 John 1:9; Heb 4:14-16; 7:25; Rom 8:34)
[98] (1 John 1:7; Eph. 1:7; Col. 1:14)

When we confess our sins in repentance, the blood of Jesus cleanses from all the effects of sin. Certainly, this should define what happens to everyone when they are born again, and it should be once for all. Even as Jesus died once for sin, we should also determine that we would have the same response[99]. We should go on to perfection and not keep re-laying the foundation of repentance from dead works (works that lead to death)[100]. Still, the goodness of God that leads us to repentance continues to work. The conviction of the Holy Spirit that convinces of sin convicts, and when sins are confessed with the purpose of forsaking them they are forgiven. There is no promise of forgiveness to those who continue on in sin. The practice of sin is condemned in the strongest language of the scripture[101]. God tells us not to have any fellowship with darkness. He tells us not to even eat with a person who calls themselves a brother if they continue practicing sin[102]. How then would we say that God has any kind of fellowship with such a one? We cannot attempt to turn the grace of God into an allowance for practicing sin and refusing the Lordship of Jesus[103]. God says,

---

[99] (Rom 6:10-11)
[100] (Heb. 6:1)
[101] (1 John 3:8-9; Hebrew 10:26; Gal. 5:21; Eph. 5:6; 1 Cor. 6:10)
[102] (1 Cor. 5:11; 2 Thess. 3:6)
[103] (Jude 4; Rom. 6:1, 3:8, 15)

> "He that covers his sins shall not prosper: but whoever confesses and forsakes them shall have mercy."
>
> (Pr. 28:13)

The mercy of God that comes to us by the grace of God supplies us with an ongoing means of forgiveness if we sin, which is found in the same way that it was first received: by repentance. This is a repentance that is displayed by confessing our sins and forsaking them. Once sin is turned from and forgiven by the applied blood of Jesus, there should be no more remembrance of them. Why? Because by the grace of God, our sins are blotted out through the forgiveness that is in Christ Jesus. James says in the context of healing and prayer that if a person sins they shall be forgiven[104]. John says that if anyone sins then he shall ask and He will give him life[105]. James also extends this into our personal relationships with one another when he says,

> "Confess your faults one to another, and pray one for another, that you may be healed."
>
> (James 5:16)

> "I acknowledged my sin unto You, And my iniquity have I not hid. I said, I will confess my transgressions

---

[104] (James 1:15b)
[105] (1 John 5:16)

unto the LORD: And You forgave the iniquity of my sin. Selah."

(Ps. 32:5)

The Blood

The shed blood of Jesus is the basis for every dimension of salvation that we have been given. If a person wants to be cleansed from their sins, there is no other Biblical concept than the cleansing provided by the atoning blood. It is the shedding of Christ Jesus' blood and the redemption that it brought to pass that defines grace. The blood of Jesus then is described as the means of forgiveness of sins, of redemption, of remission of sins, of cleansing of sins, the means by which we were purchased by God, and made righteous and holy. However, nowhere in scripture is there a guarantee that we will not sin after having been cleansed. However, we are promised that there is mercy and forgiveness with God, and that mercy and forgiveness is on the basis of the blood of Jesus.

There is certainly no question that the type in the Old Testament, the sacrifice for sin representing Jesus and His blood which has now been shed, shows that there must be a confession of sin, and then the application of the blood upon the altar to make atonement[106]. The confession of sin for forgiveness is shown in the New Testament to be the requirement for forgiveness. There is nowhere in Scripture

---

[106] (Lev. 5:5; Num. 5:7; Jer. 3:13; Lev. 16:21;)

that suggests that forgiveness is granted without first asking for it. It is impossible to be forgiven without asking for it – the concept does not exist anywhere in the Scripture. Forgiveness with God is only found by the blood of Jesus, so there must be the application of the blood to our hearts to remove a defiled conscience[107].

There is very little difference between the concept of asking for forgiveness and repenting[108]. The prophecies of Ezekiel are set in the future as well as having application of the past:

> *"The righteousness of the righteous shall not deliver him in the day of his transgression. As for the wickedness of the wicked, he shall not fall thereby in the day that he turns from his wickedness, neither shall the righteous be able to live for his righteousness in the day that he sins. When I shall say to the righteous that he shall surely live, if he trusts to his own righteousness and commits iniquity, all his righteousnesses shall not be remembered – but for his iniquity that he has committed, he shall die for it. Again, when I say unto the wicked, 'You shalt surely die,' if he turns from his sin, and does that which is lawful and right – If the wicked restore the pledge,*

---

[107] (Heb. 10:22, 12:24; 1 Pt. 1:2; cr Ex. 24:8, 29:20,21; Lev. 1:5 *etc.*; *also* Ezekiel 43:18)
[108] (Jer. 31:19; Ezek. 18:21-23, 33:12-14; Joel 2:13; Luke 15:7, 17:3; Rev. 2:5; Luke 6:37, 11:4, 17:4)

give again that he had robbed, walk in the statutes of life, without committing iniquity – he shall surely live, he shall not die. None of his sins that he has committed shall be mentioned unto him. He has done what is lawful and right – he shall surely live"

(Eze. 33:13–16).

God established the need for the confession of sins with Judah[109]; Pharaoh[110]; Moses[111]; Balaam[112]; Achan[113]; Saul[114]; David[115]; Shimei[116]; Manasseh[117]; Isaiah[118]; Jeremiah[119]; Daniel[120]; Ezra[121]; Nehemiah[122]; Job[123]; The Prodigal son[124]; Corinthian believers[125] etc. He purifies anyone who confesses sins[126], confesses faults[127], and there are also a number of places where confession is implied[128].

---

[109] (Gen. 38:26)
[110] (Ex. 10:16)
[111] (Ex. 32:30-32)
[112] (Num. 22:34)
[113] (Jos. 7:20)
[114] (1 Sam. 15:24)
[115] (2 Sam. 12:13)
[116] (2 Sam. 19:20)
[117] (2 Chron. 33:11-13)
[118] (Isa. 6:5)
[119] (Jer. 3:25)
[120] (Dan 9:20)
[121] (Ezra 10:1)
[122] (Ne. 1:6)
[123] (Job 42:6)
[124] (Luke 15:18)
[125] (1 Cor 5:1-13; 2 Cor 2:1-11, 7:9-10)
[126] (1 John 1:9)
[127] (James 5:16)
[128] (Luke 17:3-4; Eph. 4:32; and Col. 3:13, *also* Rev 2 and 3)

The New Testament calls us to die unto sin once, even as Christ Jesus died once unto sin[129]. The call to repentance is without question in the preaching of the Gospel. The repentance unto life that brings the new creation should cause us to never trespass against our God. The issue then comes to bear: what does a person do when they sin, for the wages of sin is death?[130] Is there an accountability for sin?[131] Is there any other means for sin to be cleansed other than the blood of Jesus?

It's His blood that cleanses us from all sin and nothing but the blood of Jesus. It's His blood that gives us boldness. It's the blood of the everlasting covenant that we continually rely upon as our purity and life. When a person sins against another person, there is a need to ask for forgiveness. How much more is there a need to ask God for forgiveness when we sin against Him and recognize that it's the blood that cleanses?[132] How could we think that repentance or asking for forgiveness is somehow unnecessary when it comes to trespassing against God? Is there any other means of forgiveness besides the blood of Jesus? Are we not in need of Christ Jesus every second? Surely the love that He has poured into our hearts causes us to want to please Him more than any other one in this life. With such a desire to please the

---

[129] (Rom. 6:10-12)
[130] (Rom. 6:16, 23, James 1:13-14, 2 Cor. 7:10; Rev. 2 etc..)
[131] (1 Peter 1:17; Rev. 3:19-20)
[132] (Mt. 18:15-17; Lk. 11:4; 1 John 1:9)

Lord, when we do something that is displeasing, surely we would find ourselves broken and repentant. It's only his blood and faith in the blood that would remove the guilty conscience caused by trespassing against the most wonderful and Holy God. The blood that purifies and has cleansed us is all our boldness to interact with Him.

While God's preserving power keeps us and His mercy gives us a space of time to repent, if we sin, we are to confess our sins[133].

> "Sin interrupts, but confession restores that fellowship. Immediate confession keeps the fellowship unbroken."
>
> (C. I. Scofield, 1917)

> "It imports such a confession as was made by the high-priest on the great day of annual expiation, when he laid his hands on the scape-goat, and confessed over him all the sins of all the children of Israel, whilst all of those whose sins he so transferred were 'afflicting their souls before God.' … I may add, that this *confession implies also a forsaking of the sins so confessed.*"
>
> (Charles Simeon, 1833)

> "This will do much more toward advancing our relationship with God than ignoring our sin, as the

---

[133] (1 John 1:9; James 5:15; Hebrews 10:19-22)

separatists advocate. Sincere confession has a sure result: forgiveness."

(William R. Baker and Paul K. Carrier, 1990)

Below are the redemptive words that are associated with the blood of the covenant and forgiveness. God has placed all the power of life, redemption, forgiveness, cleansing and being made righteous in the blood of His only begotten Son Jesus:

1. **Forgiveness**: ἄφεσις ('aphesis,' release, erase, remission, remit)
   - Blood of the covenant for <u>removal</u> of sins[134].
   - In whom we have redemption through His blood, the <u>forgiveness</u> of sins, according to the riches of his grace;[135]
   - In Whom we have redemption through His blood, even the <u>forgiveness</u> of sins,[136]
   - And almost all things are by the Law purged with blood, and without shedding of blood there is no <u>remission</u>[137].
   - Now where <u>remission</u> of these is, there is no more offering for sin[138].

---

[134] (Mt. 26:28)
[135] (Eph. 1:6–7)
[136] (Col. 1:14)
[137] (Heb. 9:22)
[138] (Heb. 10:18)

2. **Redemption**: λυτρόω ('lutroo,' set free, ransom, liberate) can be regarded as a lexical synonym to ἄφεσις
   - <u>redeemed</u> by the blood[139].
   - Who gave Himself for us, that He might <u>redeem</u> us from all iniquity, and purify unto Himself a peculiar people, zealous for good works[140].

3. **Remission**: πάρεσις ('paresis,' passing over, letting go, dismissal)
   - Whom God has set forth to be a propitiation through faith in His blood, to declare His righteousness for the <u>remission</u> of sins that are past, through the forbearance of God[141].

4. **Cleanses**: καθαρίζω ('katharizo,' makes clean, purifies, undefiled)
   - But if we walk in the light, as He is in the light, we have fellowship one with another, and the blood of Jesus Christ His Son <u>cleanses</u> us from all sin[142].
   - How much more shall the blood of Christ, Who through the eternal Spirit offered Himself without spot to God, <u>purge</u> your conscience from dead works to serve the living God?[143]

---

[139] (1 Peter 1:19, Col 1:14)
[140] (Tt 2:14)
[141] (Rom. 3:24–25)
[142] (1 Jn. 1:7)
[143] (Heb. 9:13–14)

5. **Purchased**: περιποιέω ('peripoieo,' obtain, acquire, save, procure)
    - Take heed therefore unto yourselves, and to all the flock, over which the Holy Ghost has made you overseers, to feed the church of God, which He has <u>purchased</u> with His own blood[144].

6. **Made Righteous**: δικαιόω ('dikaioo,' make right, justify, justice, just, righteous, pronounce righteous)
    - Much more then, being now <u>justified</u> by His blood, we shall be saved from wrath through Him[145].

---

[144] (Acts 20:28)
[145] (Rom. 5:8-9)

The Covenant of Blood is a Covenant of Grace Fully Revealed

The covenant of the Law was powerless to impart the life of God. This is beyond dispute, because the Apostle Paul says,

> "If a Law had been given that had power to give life, then righteousness would have indeed come by the Law."
>
> (Gal. 3:21)

The New Covenant, by contrast, imparted life. What life did it impart? Our Lord says, "I am the life" (John 11:25, 14:6). Is there any life apart from God?

> "And this is the witness that God has given us: eternal life – and this life is in His Son. He who has the Son has life, and he who does not have the Son of God does not have life."
>
> (1 John 5:11-12)

God gave us His life by giving us His Son. He gave us His life by giving us His own blood, which alone has the power to destroy sin. He gave us His life by giving us His own Spirit of Holiness.

The covenant of the Law could not result in a change of nature, because it could not impart His life. Therefore, the person under the covenant of the Law desired to do good, but sin was at work within him. The bondage of sin and death had established dominion over mankind because of Adam's transgression. Through Christ Jesus, the dominion of sin and death was destroyed and a New Covenant was established in the blood of Jesus, the covenant of blood[146]. The blood that washed away and loosed us from our sins had to be supplied by "the Word made flesh," the ultimate act of grace (John 1:14). The New Covenant that imparted the life of God could only come by God's only begotten Son. This great gift of God's grace became a flood of God's life springing up and flooding out in anyone who would believe.

Whereas the first covenant of the Law was as a schoolmaster showing man his sin and God's disposition towards it[147], the New Covenant is the removal of sin[148]. Now that we are cleansed, made holy, and pure, God is at work on the inside developing and maturing us in all of His ways[149].

---

[146] (Mt. 26:28, Rom. 8:3, Heb. 10:29, 13:20)
[147] (Gal. 3:24-27)
[148] (Col. 2:11-12)
[149] (Eph. 3:20, 2 Cor. 4:7, Eph. 1:19)

> *"It is God Who works in you both to will and to do His good pleasure."*
>
> (Php. 2:13)

With God at work in us, how can we be defeated? God dwells in us and we dwell in Him and we rely on Him to do all that pleases Him.

> *"And this is how we know that we dwell in Him, and He in us, by the Spirit that He has given us."*
>
> (1 John 4:13)

> *"Whoever confesses that Jesus is the Son of God, God dwells in him, and he in God."*
>
> (1 John 4:15)

This is the New Covenant, "Christ in you" (Col. 1:27).

The Law was the ministry of condemnation, but the New Covenant of Grace is the ministry of righteousness[150]. The Law was the ministry of condemnation, because sin still had dominion, but the New Covenant is the ministry of righteousness, because the dominion of sin is removed, and God dwells within. The Law was a schoolmaster, but grace gave us sonship[151]. The Covenant of the Law was written on tables of stone, but the Covenant of Grace was written on the tables of our heart and mind[152].

---

[150] (2 Cor. 3:9)
[151] (Gal. 3:23-29)
[152] (2 Cor. 3:3)

Everyone should be able to agree that God gave us a New Covenant, one that is complete and final, in which He wrote the laws and ways of God upon the table of our hearts and minds[153]. This New Covenant is a Covenant of Grace because it no longer depends on man's ability in an unregenerate state[154]. It no longer relies upon the weakness of human ability – because the Holy Spirit now has come to dwell within us, God is at work. Now by His Word and by His Spirit, we learn – not from a schoolmaster, but from the Spirit of life – how to walk as God walks[155]. The very life and power of God dwells within, and now God walks out His life through us[156]. This is grace, a covenant that does not depend upon the flesh (mans' ability), but rather God's ability, which is imparted to us with His life.

The first time that the phrase "New Covenant" is used is in Jer. 31:31. Jeremiah set the precedence for what the New Covenant would be,

> "'Behold, the days come,' says the LORD, 'that I will make a **new covenant** with the house of Israel, and with the house of Judah – not according to the covenant that I made with their fathers in the day that I took them by the hand to bring them out of the

---

[153] (2 Cor. 3:3, Heb. 8:10, 10:16)
[154] (Rom. 8:3)
[155] (Gal. 3)
[156] (2 Cor. 6:18)

*land of Egypt – forasmuch as they broke My covenant, although I was a lord over them,' says the LORD. 'But this is the covenant that I will make with the house of Israel after those days,' says the LORD, '**I will put My law in their inward parts, and in their heart will I write it;** and I will be their God, and they shall be My people; and they shall teach no more every man his neighbor, and every man his brother, saying, "Know the LORD"; for they shall all know Me, from the least of them unto the greatest of them,' says the LORD; 'for I will forgive their iniquity, and their sin will I remember no more.'"*

(Jeremiah 31:31-34)

Grace and truth came by Jesus Christ[157] and from Him we have received grace upon grace[158]. This grace is all about the power of sin and death being destroyed and the ways of God being established in our inner being. This grace that we have received is Christ in us our confidence of glory[159]. We did not receive His life in part, but He stepped in with the fullness of His Spirit[160]. What He has was given to us in full[161]: His life, His righteousness, His holiness, and His relationship with God as Father.

---

[157] (John 1:17)
[158] (John 1:16)
[159] (Col. 1:27; John 17:22, 2 Peter 1:3)
[160] (Eph. 3:19, Col. 2:9)
[161] (Rom. 8:32)

Grace: The Door has been open to All

"Believers are in Him before God, not in what they do or according to their service, or anything else, but in perfection of what He is. Who could add to His fullness and who can add to the fullness and completeness the believer possesseth forever in Him!"

(Arno C. Gaebelein, 2009).

That grace is fundamentally revealed in that He has come and we have received Him, and having received Him, we received the authority to be the sons of God, because we believed upon His name[162]. Paul further defined this sonship when he said that as many as are led by the Spirit, the Spirit of Holiness, are the sons of God[163]. As the sons of God we are heirs and joint heirs together with Him[164]. As sons we are given the full rights of fellowship and ultimately to be glorified with His glory and see Him as He is[165]. With such an expectation, we purify ourselves even as He is pure[166].

There are three outstanding covenants highlighted in the New Testament: the covenant of circumcision, the covenant of the Law and the New Covenant in His blood. All of them involved the initiative of God in which He made a pledge of His redemption to man. The covenant of

---

[162] (John 1:12)
[163] (Rom. 8:14)
[164] (Rom. 8:17, Gal. 4:7, Tit. 3:7)
[165] (1 Jn. 3:1-2)
[166] (1 Jn. 3:3; 2 Cor 7:1)

circumcision centered around the promise that God made concerning His Seed, Who would redeem man with His own blood. The Law, which was a schoolmaster, would train His people that sin was exceedingly sinful, but had to be removed so that a true fellowship could be established between God and man. Both of these covenants were acts of God's grace, because God was acting to bring about what only He could do. The Greek word for covenant is found 33 times in the New Testament. However, the exact phrase "Covenant of Grace" is never found. We observe that the Covenant of the Law is set in contrast to Grace, and from that derive the concept of the Covenant of Grace[167].

It was not until mankind received the new heart and the new spirit that the New Covenant could be witnessed, and this would come about by the ultimate act of God's grace. God became flesh. He became the Intercessor for man, and by His own power would take on the sin that men had submitted themselves to, and by Himself He would defeat the stronghold and deliver all who would trust Him from the prison of sin and death. It must be understood in terms of the blood of Jesus, and what the blood has done for us, and what it means now and also in the future.

---

[167] (Rom. 6:14, Eph. 2:8-10)

The blood removed our sins[168]. The blood is how we come boldly into the Holy of Holies[169], and the means by which we are cleansed through the intercession of Christ Jesus[170]. It is by the blood of Jesus that we will be found spotless on the day of judgment and be presented as priests and kings to God and our Father[171]. While we rely on the absolute obedience of Christ for all that we have in God, we give ourselves to being conformed to His image[172]. The great grace that God has provided for us is to unite us with Himself "that as He is, so are we now in this world."[173]

One of the most obvious and fundamental meanings of Covenant is "an agreement." God has given us His Covenant of love and we must be willing to agree. One of the meanings for a Hebrew word חֶסֶד ('chesed'), usually translated as "mercy" or "lovingkindness," is "covenant love." 'Chesed' is almost inseparable from the meaning of grace. It is argued by some that covenant love is the primary meaning for 'chesed.' What is certain is that there are few words or phrases that could more perfectly express the covenant of God than a Covenant of Love.

The covenants of God are discovered in the relationship that God had with Abraham. These are the

---

[168] (Mt. 26:27-28)
[169] (Heb. 10:19)
[170] (Eph. 1:7, Heb. 9:14, 10:19-22, 1 John 1:7, Rev. 1:5)
[171] (Rev. 1:5-6)
[172] (Rom. 8:29, 1 John 2:6, 4:12)
[173] (1 Jn. 4:17; Rom. 6:14-23)

most amazing oath covenants that can be thought of: God swearing and pledging Himself to a man! There are those who have sought to place greater constraints of obligation upon God based on His covenants. However, a covenant cuts both ways. The example of relationship on the other side is the obedience of Abraham, that whether it is grace or faith, it was an obedience out of love.

God did not extend His righteousness to Abraham solely on the basis of Abraham's obedience, though it was an obedience that went beyond any others that we know. He extended it solely on the basis of relationship – on the basis of His love for Abraham. Abraham was willing to believe in the coming Seed, the one who alone would provide righteousness for all. God did not see Himself indebted to Abraham, and so righteousness was not given based on debt, rather God had found a man that would agree with Him. As God passed between those pieces of the sacrifice in the glory and fire of His goodness, He made a promise that Abraham agreed with. Through the miraculous oath of God Abraham entered the most amazing relationship possible: a deeper relationship with God. God has brought us into the covenant that He made through His Son, an oath that extends way beyond that which He made with Abraham. It does not matter how obedient or how righteous a man is, no one could ever be worthy of the holiness and righteousness of God. Mankind, bound by the disobedience and sin of Adam, remained in bondage to Adam's sin and death until the true holy and righteous One came to offer His life as a ransom. He ransomed us providing us with the ability to be born back into the family of God. He crowned us with His lovingkindness and put His Spirit within us, clothing us with His righteousness and holiness.

Through the blood of the everlasting covenant, God extended His life to all who will agree. Anyone who will come and eat His flesh and drink His blood receives this life of God. We partake of Him and are made one with Him, He dwells in us and we dwell in Him[174]. Men – dead in their trespasses and sins, separated by wicked works – must only agree with the covenant of God. This covenant belongs to anyone who will believe[175]. God will not justify the wicked, but has provided a means for all the ungodly to receive His righteousness: all they must do is agree with the covenant and the miracle of a changed life will take place. In this, God's righteousness is not just accounted to them, it is placed within them by the new creation. God steps inside and takes up His dwelling in us and we are made a new man, recreated in God's image and likeness.

---

[174] (John 6:56; 14:17-23; 1 John 3:24; 4:15-16)
[175] (John 3:15-16; John 6:47; Mark 16:16; Rom 10:11, etc…)

Brief History of the Theology of Grace

The message of grace within Christian theology has changed over the centuries. Prior to Augustine, who lived in the 4th century, it was formulated that grace was the divine decrees that were received on the conditions of faith and obedience. Then came Augustine and the debate with Pelagius. In Augustine's zeal to oppose in every way the notions of Pelagius, Augustine sought to enhance the glory of grace. He then put forth that God chooses to save unconditionally those whom He wills. However, he did not teach the doctrine that some men were also created only for destruction (doctrine of unconditional reprobation). The doctrine of unconditional reprobation was not taught until the 9th century. It was Calvin who, in the 16th century, embraced the unconditional reprobation doctrines taught by Gottschalk from the 9th century. It was Calvin who began to teach the most radical versions of unconditional election and reprobation. Calvin built his whole theology upon this foundation. He interpreted all the Word of God on this preconceived notion. On the other hand, Martin Luther held to the long-espoused doctrine of conditional election which was more in keeping with the pre-Augustinian views of grace. Whereas, Calvin taught "irresistible" or "special" grace that was given by God only to the elect: those who God decided should be saved.

In the 16th century, Jacob Arminius (1560-1609), who was taught by Theodore Beza at the Geneva school, stepped forward to refute the doctrines of Calvin. Arminius became devoted to proving that the doctrines of Calvin which were taught by Beza – of divine predestination as unconditional, and the immutable decree of God concerning the salvation or damnation of each individual – did not correctly define divine grace and were contrary to Scripture (Mark Galli and Ted Olsen, 2000). Arminius argued that these doctrines unjustly made God the Author of sin. He argued that grace was not irresistible, for it was said of many that they resisted the Holy Spirit[176]. Arminius insisted that

> "Grace is not a synonym for 'decree' or 'will' or 'sovereignty'; grace is God's love addressing humans in their depravity rather than 'affecting' them as creatures without reference to their sin"
> (V. Shepherd, "Arminius, Jacobus," ed. Timothy Larsen et al., 2003).

---

[176] (Acts 7:51)

He refuted Calvin's doctrine at almost every point. Arminius was said to have been "one of the most learned men of a learned age." Neander called him the "model of a conscientious and zealously investigating theologian" (History of Dogmas, ii, 276)

(McClintock and Strong Biblical Cyclopedia Online). Arminius taught that justification originates solely by the grace of God and regarded election to eternal life as being on the condition of faith in Christ, but not omitting obedience to God as an act of faith. Arminius taught that men have a free will and that primary or "prevenient" (preparatory) grace results in an individual being able to cooperate with God in salvation. Arminius also taught that Christ Jesus suffered for everyone, emphasizing that grace could be resisted. Today,

> "Arminian doctrine is found in widely diversified groups: Lutherans, Methodists, Episcopalians, Anglicans, Pentecostalists, Free Will Baptists, and most charismatic and holiness believers."
>
> (Paul P. Enns, 1989)

So much of the church is divided between either understanding the Scripture based on Calvin's theories or the writings of Arminius. Every person should use caution that they are not reading Scripture through those concepts imposed upon them by the theological indoctrination that they have been exposed to. Reading the Scripture and understanding it purely on the basis of what is written should not be looked down upon, but encouraged. Understanding the thoughts of the Patristics who wrote Homilies prior to Augustine are also valuable insight as to how the Scripture was received and understood in the times closer to the 1st century church.

Faith is Our Response to God

"For by grace are you saved through faith, and that not of ourselves- it is the gift of God"

(Eph. 2:8)

Grace that has appeared to all men draws us to the place where we are redeemed: the cross of Christ. Grace works the miracle of faith, which is the new birth. It's not by any works of our own righteousness but by His mercy we were washed and made a new creation[177]. Grace brings the Holy Spirit into our lives who teaches us to deny ungodliness and worldly lust and to live righteously, godly and soberly in this present world[178]. The Holy Spirit opens our spiritual eyes to see Jesus and what He has done for us and faith is born in our hearts[179]. Faith becomes our participation with what only God can do. Faith is our response to the work of the Holy Spirit who draws us to Jesus[180]. Through the faith that we were given by the Holy Spirit we say, "yes," to God's work of salvation, and God does the rest. Christ Jesus draws all men unto the place

---

[177] (Titus 3:5)
[178] (Titus 2:11)
[179] (Acts 26:18; 2 Cor. 4:4; Jn. 8:12; Lk. 1:79)
[180] (John 6:44, 12:32; Acts 2:21, 39)

where He died for us at Calvary so that we might receive the free gift of His love: salvation[181]. Through faith we are kept by the power of God[182]. Faith is our response to God's gift of grace and is described in terms of obedience. In fact, faith defines the relationship between God and man[183].

The very first lesson in Scripture shows us the impact of obedience to God. Adam was given one simple command from God: not to eat of the Tree of the Knowledge of Good and Evil. Their disobedience resulted in sin entering into the world. Their disobedience brought all men under the bondage of sin and death. Their disobedience resulted in spiritual death. Their disobedience broke trust with God. Thus the potency of disobedience was underscored even beyond words. Trusting God is the foundation of faith. It is the Old Testament foundation for the Apostles Paul thesis on, "the righteous live by faith" (Hab. 2:4; Rom. 1:17). Trusting Him, relying upon Him, faith in Him will ultimately result in perfect obedience to Him. God is correct in all of His judgments. He alone knows the ways of life, and all of His commandments are to teach us how to walk in them so that we may live His kind of life.

The second great lesson that we have on obedience is the obedience of Abraham. The relationship between

---

[181] (Jn. 12:32; Rom. 5:15; Heb. 2:9)
[182] (1 Pet. 1:5)
[183] (Heb. 11:6)

Abraham and God began when Abraham was still living among the idolatry of the Chaldeans. We don't know what Abraham's life was like before God called Him, but we know that when God called him, Abraham obeyed. It was not an easy task, because Abraham left his home and all that was familiar to him not knowing where he was going[184]. God began training Abraham that He was trustworthy. After Abraham had gone through many challenging situations, he received even a greater promise from God. The ultimate promise was that the Seed, the Messiah, would be one of His descendants. Abraham believed God concerning the Seed – which Paul revealed was Christ Jesus – and it was accounted to Abraham for righteousness[185]. That promise was ultimately confirmed when Abraham obeyed God and took Isaac up to Moriah to offer him as a sacrifice to God[186]. In many respects that is the ultimate example of trusting God. Abraham came to know God and was assured that God was able also to raise Him up after he offered Isaac up[187].

Obedience is not a peripheral subject to the relationship between God and man. Rather, obedience is at the very heart of our relationship with God. **Obedience is the expression of faith**[188]. The word obedience

---

[184] (Heb. 11:8)
[185] (Gen. 15:6; Gal. 3:16)
[186] (Gen. 22:2, 5, 12, 17-18)
[187] (Gen. 22:5; Heb. 11:17-19)
[188] (James 2:20-26; Heb. 11:1-40)

(including obey) is found about 150 times in the Bible. Every promise and blessing of God in both the Old Testament and the New Testament are conditional based upon obedience, which is underscored by the "if" (used 1500 times) that occurs with every one of God's promises and blessings. Believing what God says has some expression of obedience. The reward of obedience is that we become the elect of God because we have obeyed[189]. We are made righteous, holy and acceptable by the Holy Spirit. We inherit all the many benefits and blessings of the gift of salvation. Trusting God and living in the faith that He has given, we become obedient children, not to fashioning ourselves in any way after the lust of the world – but as God is Holy, we are to be holy[190].

Paul instructs us to be obedient to the faith. We are to be the servants of God by obedience unto righteousness[191]. He says that it was by his ministry that God made the nations obedient in word and in works[192]. Revelation of the mystery of God was made known to all the world through obedience to the faith[193]. The call of God for everyone of us is to walk in the obedience of Jesus Christ, and it was to this end that the grace of God has provided us with all things in salvation[194]. God in His love

---
[189] (Rom. 6:17; 1 Pet. 1:22; Heb. 11:6)
[190] (1 Pet. 1:2, 14-15)
[191] (Rom. 6:16)
[192] (Rom. 15:18)
[193] (Rom. 16:26)
[194] (2 Cor. 10:4-5)

and mercy is longsuffering with us. He lovingly guides us and trains us in all of His ways. These ways of God that have been foreign to us, God devotes Himself to teach us. He leads us and trains us as a loving father. If we are willing, we will learn perfect obedience because there is nothing better than His ways. When we discover who He is and what He desires for our life, we also discover there is nothing better. There is no love like His love. There are no ways like His ways. His ways are so much better than any others. The grace of God reveals to us the beauty of God and also empowers us to live His kind of life. We learn step by step through obedience. As we obey God, we come to understand why He has asked certain things of us that at first we may have not understood.

Although there are many other great examples of obedience, none can compare to the obedience of Christ Jesus, Who learned obedience by the things that He suffered[195]. It was through the obedience of One, Christ Jesus, that many are made righteous[196]. Very specifically, the righteousness that we now possess is the righteousness of God that came to us through Christ Jesus' obedience. Jesus was shown to be the Son of God by the Spirit of Holiness, and today, as the sons of God, we have been given the same Spirit[197]. It is through the faith of the Lord

---

[195] (Heb. 5:8)
[196] (Rom. 5:19)
[197] (Rom. 1:3)

Jesus Christ that each one of us are empowered to enjoy His life and obedience.

Grace has gifted us and empowered us with the ability to have the proper response to all that God has asked of us. Grace is the gift, and faith is our response; and, most importantly, the gift is not of ourselves – it is the gift of God. Once again, without faith it is impossible to please God. When we look at faith in the context of Enoch, we observe his walk, his relationship, and his obedience to God. The walk that he had with God is all about the relationship that he had with God. The relationship that Enoch had with God pleased God, and so we know it was a faith-walk[198]. In fact, in many ways Hebrews 11:6 is defined in terms of the walk that Enoch had with God,

> *"By faith Enoch was translated that he should not see death, and was not found, because God had translated him: for before his translation he had this testimony: that he pleased God. But without faith it is impossible to please Him – for he that comes to God must believe that He is, and that He is a rewarder of them who diligently seek Him."*
>
> (Heb. 11:5–6)

Enoch's faith-walk distinguished him from all of the wickedness that surrounded him in his generation. We

---

[198] (Heb. 11:6)

only have one sermon handed down to us concerning the way that Enoch walked with God and it is found in Jude,

> *"And Enoch also, the seventh from Adam, prophesied of these, saying, 'Behold, the Lord comes with ten thousands of his saints, to execute judgment upon all, and to convince all that are ungodly among them of all their ungodly deeds which they have ungodly committed, and of all their hard speeches which ungodly sinners have spoken against Him'"*
> (Jude 1:14–15).

The one outstanding thing about his prophecy is that ungodliness was something that he knew was detested by God and had God's judgment upon it.

The Apostle Paul unequivocally associated believing with obedience and unbelief with disobedience. The place that this is exemplified the most is in his epistle to the Hebrews. Paul describes the disobedience of Israel in the wilderness as unbelief. The evil heart of unbelief that Paul describes is the disobedience that we read about in Exodus and Numbers. Their disobedience was attributed to not knowing the ways of God[199]. That disobedience and unbelief is made very pointed when it is directed to us, exhorting us not to depart from the living God[200]. Such a departure exemplifies not only unbelief but the ultimate

---

[199] (Heb. 3:10)
[200] (Heb. 3:12)

act of disobedience. It is further elucidated as disobedience by pointing out that it is the deceitfulness of sin that produces such a state[201]. It was with them who sinned that God was grieved, and sin and disobedience are one and the same[202]. It was because of sin that God rejected them, and it was this disobedience and continual rejection of God's instructions that God called unbelief[203].

It's a tragic thing to consider that many walk in this same kind of disobedience and refuse to be corrected. There are those who have departed from the faith and obedience toward God and don't know it, because their doctrine of God describes otherwise, but like Samson, the Lord has departed from them and they do not know it [204]. It's hard to imagine how man would let the holiness and purity of God become so absent from their minds that they would think that they were right with God while living in ungodliness. They would make Jesus the Minister of sin by describing the salvation that came by Him as some form of remedy that made sin acceptable to God. This kind of thinking is not the faith that was once delivered unto the saints: the faith that has called us to holiness and obedience[205].

---

[201] (Heb. 3:13)
[202] (Heb. 3:17)
[203] (Heb. 3:18-19)
[204] (Judges 16:20; 2 Peter 2:1; Jude 1:4; cr. 1 Samuel 6:14)
[205] (Jude 1:1-25)

Ignatius of Antioch, one of the martyrs of the church, wrote in his letter to the church at Ephesus expressing the gospel that was most certainly accepted in his day,

> "No man [truly] making a profession of faith sins, nor does he who possesses love hate anyone. The tree is made manifest by its fruit, so those who profess themselves to be Christians shall be recognized by their conduct. For there is not now a demand for mere profession, but that a man be found continuing in the power of faith to the end."

Ignatius was thrown to the lions, because he was known as the one who carried about within him He Who was crucified. The message of obedience to God and the indwelling of Christ Jesus, and not merely a life imputed, was most certainly believed by the 2nd century church.

> "For, 'by grace you are saved,' he says, 'through faith.' Then, so as to do no injury to free will, he allots a role to us, then takes it away again, saying, 'and this not of ourselves.'"
>
> (Chrysostom, Homily on Ephesians 4.2.8)

Salvation For Anyone and Everyone: The Whole World

It is said that the whole of doctrine and Christian theology is embraced in three terms: God's nature, man's nature, and the interaction of the two. Thus, who is God? Who is man? And what is the intended relationship between them? God created Adam and Eve after His likeness and image. He created them in splendor and glory, and He gave them dominion over the works of His hands. This is how God introduced Himself and the man that He created, as well as the relationship that He proposed to have with Him. It is therefore right to build the whole of our theology around this revealed plan of God for man. The first two chapters of Genesis allow us to behold what God intended. The first chapter of John allows us to see how God restored it.

When Adam rebelled, God immediately went to work to rescue him, to provide a covering and a promise for a cure to his disobedience through a coming Redeemer. It was there on that day that man sinned that the Seed was promised and God gave His Only Begotten Son. He did not utterly forsake them, but continued to interact with the fallen man and his offspring. Out of them arose an Abel, an Enoch, and a Noah, all men of faith. Abel was the first to demonstrate proper worship, Enoch pleased God, and Noah was found righteous. Down through the ages, God has had close intimate relationships with men like Abraham who received God's promise – also Job, who God called perfect and upright. God had Moses and Joshua, who were willing to walk with Him. He had Samuel, David, Elijah, and many more. In all of God's dealings with mankind, He has revealed those whom He was pleased with and the kind of relationship that He desires to have. He has revealed His nature: that He is merciful and gracious, longsuffering, and full of lovingkindness and truth. God is holy and consecrated to His purity. He has nothing to do with sin in any way. The full expression of His holiness is His love, a love that works no ill toward anyone. God fully revealed His nature in Christ Jesus, Who was the full expression of God the Father. He showed us that God, Who so loved the world, was also willing to lay His life down for every man that comes into the world[206].

God chose Abraham, who in obedience to Him offered his son Isaac, and he received a great reward of God's promise. Through Abraham, a family was chosen and consecrated to bring forth the Redeemer for the whole world. This was not to eliminate all others by choosing

---

[206] (John 1:9)

only one family, but that the Redeemer might come to save all nations and families of men. Men distort the scriptures like those found in Romans 9 & 11 to make salvation only for a few predetermined people chosen by God in the eternal past[207]. Rather, God elected that all men should be saved. He predetermined a plan of salvation and not the individuals in that plan. He determined that he would have a Seed and choose the family and individuals through whom His Seed would come.

God so loved the world that He gave His only begotten Son for anyone who would believe[208]. If salvation were limited to a few predetermined individuals, the Scripture would plainly say so. However, it does not – the door of salvation is open to anyone who will respond to God. God made Adam and Eve and after they fell He chose to redeem them and all of their descendants if they desired. Christ Jesus gives the opportunity for anyone who believes to be saved. Jesus said that He would draw all men unto Himself[209]. Paul said that the grace of God that brings salvation has appeared to all men[210]. He said that God would have all men to be saved and come to the knowledge of the truth[211]. Peter said that God is not

---
[207] (2 Pet. 3:16)
[208] (John 3:16-17, Rom. 5:8, 18, 2 Cor. 5:14-15, 1 Tim. 2:4, 4:10, Heb. 2:9, 10:29, 2 Pet. 2:1, 1 John 2:2, 4:14)
[209] (John 12:32)
[210] (Titus 2:11)
[211] (1 Tim. 2:4)

willing that anyone perish, but that all should come to repentance[212]. John said that Jesus died not for our sins only, but for the sins of the whole world[213].

---

[212] (2 Pet. 3:9)
[213] (1 John 2:3)

Jesus Gave the Opportunity to Anyone and Everyone to Be Saved

Jesus said,

"Behold I stand at the door and knock. If any man hears my voice and opens the door, I will come in…"

(Rev. 3:20).

In the Greek Bible, Jesus often used the word πᾶς ('pas'), which is translated as "whosoever." He never limited His invitation to just a few, but opened the door to all mankind everywhere. It's men who put limits and constraints on who can be saved, not God. Jesus and His disciples said:

- "Whosoever will confess Me before men, I will confess before My Father."
- "Whosoever will do the will of my Father in Heaven is My brother and My sister and mother."

- "Whosoever will lose his life for My sake shall find it."
- "Whosoever receives Me receives the One Who sent Me."
- "Whosoever believes in Him will not perish, but have everlasting life."
- "Whosoever drinks of this water that I shall give will never thirst again, but the water that I give shall be a spring of water springing up into everlasting life."
- "Whosoever believes in Me will not abide in darkness."
- "Whosoever shall call on the name of the Lord shall be saved."
- "Whosoever believes in Him shall receive remission of sins."
- "Whosoever believes in Him shall not be ashamed."
- "Whosoever shall call upon the name of the Lord shall be saved."
- "Whosoever shall confess that Jesus is the Son of God, God dwells in him and he in God"[214]

---

[214] (Mt. 10:32, 12:50, 16:25; Mark 10:15; Luke 6:47, 9:48; John 3:15,16, 4:14, 12:46; Acts 2:21, 10:43; Romans 9:33, 10:11,13; 1 John 4:15; 2 Cor. 5:14-15; 1 Tim. 2:4, 4:10; Heb. 2:9, 10:29; 2 Pet. 2:1,; 1 John 2:2, 4:14)

Christ Jesus died for all so that all men might be saved[215]. He poured out His blood for the whole world[216]. Jesus became the Lamb of God to take away the sins of the world[217]. He is the Savior of the world[218]. Jesus tasted death for every man[219]. There are no limitations to a select group of people that God decided to save in the eternal past. There is no group of people pointed out in Scripture that He has created for destruction.

The election of God does not limit God's salvation to a select few – Paul never implied that. He argued that God's salvation includes all mankind through the sacrifice of His only begotten Son. This was God's choice of how He would save. As much as God elected that Esau the elder would serve Jacob the younger, He has elected all men to salvation, not just the Jews[220]. God's choice in Jacob was proven out, for God had to judge Esau and his descendants for the wickedness and rebellion of both[221].

Likewise, God saw that the Jews were going to continue to rebel against Him and so Paul warned them with the most severe language by implication that they would receive the same fate. There is no unrighteousness with God. He is not going to judge someone for

---

[215] (2 Cor. 5:14-15)
[216] (1 John 2:3)
[217] (John 1:29)
[218] (John 4:42)
[219] (Heb. 2:9)
[220] (Gen. 25:23; Rom. 9:13)
[221] (Obd. 1:10-16, Malachi 1:3)

something that they did not do. God in His judgment had to set Israel aside because of their persistent rebellion, and He raised up those who would bring forth the fruits of the kingdom[222]. The Jews were still trying to hang onto their own ways and ideas of the Law and refused to obey God – as a result, their hearts continued to be hardened against God. God, as the sovereign Almighty, laid down the terms of mercy and compassion. He had endured long with Israel, showing mercy and compassion to the rebellious among them for centuries, but the time of judgment had come. Just as God dealt with the rebellious Pharaoh, and through his hardened response had shown great signs and wonders, even so through the hardened hearts of Israel God would show His great power in the redemption of all the world. The hardness of Pharaoh's heart resulted in the death of the firstborn, and likewise the hardness of Israel resulted in the death of the firstborn. Through their persistent stubbornness and hardness of heart they crucified the Redeemer and rejected the Firstborn as a blasphemer, displaying the ultimate hardness of heart. Through it, God displayed His signs and wonders by the resurrection of His Firstborn.

God is not to be blamed for the disobedience and rebellion of men. God gave men the power of choice, and has shown mercy on those that He would show mercy. God chose Isaac over Ishmael, Jacob over Esau, Israel over

---

[222] (Mt. 21:33-35)

the Egyptians, and the righteous over the wickedness of Israel. Paul showed that just as God chose in the past, He now had chosen to cut Israel off. As He chose Jacob, the younger over the firstborn Esau, he now would choose the nations over Israel. Thus God hardens the heart in a similar manner to the way that He shows mercy. If men resist, He hardens them. If they respond to correction, then He shows mercy. God endured for a long time with the vessels fit for destruction in Israel. He showed mercy on top of mercy for centuries, but judgment time had come. He turned to the nations and called unto them before they had the ability to call out for Him – this is grace[223]. There is nothing about this message to the rebellious Jews that Paul has given that has anything to do with some being born for salvation and some for destruction. Such a conclusion is in direct contradiction to the rest of the New Testament and misses the point altogether.

Similarly, we must understand what Paul is saying with respect to the election of grace. We have already listed the many scriptures saying that the election of God chooses to save all who will believe. Those who respond are defined as the elect. God certainly did not choose Abraham or Moses on the basis of works – He called them, and they answered. When we consider those that God blinded, we come to understand more about the judgment that

---
[223] (Rom 9:26)

resulted in their sin. God told the prophet Isaiah to prophesy to a wicked and rebellious house who refused to obey Him,

> "And He said, 'Go, and tell this people, "Hear indeed, but understand not. And see indeed, but perceive not. Make the heart of this people fat, and make their ears heavy, and shut their eyes, lest they see with their eyes and hear with their ears and understand with their heart and be turned and be healed"'"
>
> (Isa. 6:9-10).

Later, God said to the same hard-hearted people that were still as bent on doing things their way in the days of Paul,

> "For the Lord has poured out upon you the spirit of deep sleep, and has closed your eyes – the prophets and your rulers, the seers he has covered"
>
> (Is. 29:10).

It did not matter how God sought to awaken them – they refused to respond, and thus He suffered long with the vessels fit for destruction[224]. Just as the day of reckoning had come in the time of Isaiah, even so the time had come to judge that wicked and rebellious generation that refused to hear. Now their chastening would be more severe than before, for the day of reckoning had come and

---

[224] (Rom. 9:22)

they were cut off[225]. Also, prior to all these events, God spoke to Israel in the days that they were in the wilderness concerning their continued rebellion and unwillingness to obey and said,

> "Yet the LORD has not given you a heart to perceive, and eyes to see, and ears to hear, unto this day"
>
> (Dt. 29:4).

Why? Because they refused to respond to God. There were those like Moses and Joshua who did have eyes to see and ears to hear, but those who were disobedient continued in their spiritual blindness.

Regarding all that we have said, Chrysostom also gives witness that what Paul said in Rom 9 & 11 were in fact squarely aimed at rebellious Jews that Paul labored to win. Regarding the election of grace and those who God would show mercy upon in Israel, Chrysostom writes,

> "Wherefore he proceeds to say, 'Even so then at this present time also, there is a remnant according to the election of grace.' Observe that each word maintains its own rank, showing at once God's grace, and the obedient temper of them that receive salvation. For by saying election, he showed the

---

[225] (Rom. 11:15-22)

approval of them, but by saying grace, he showed the gift of God"

(John Chrysostom, Homilie Epistle of St. Paul to the Romans).

Free Will and The Sovereignty of God

God, in His goodness and grace, gave to us the amazing life of His likeness and image. He gave us the ability to make choices and to choose to be His friend and companion. Free will is simply the choice that God has given to each person to agree with Him or not. Free will allows us to choose the things that God has chosen or to choose something different. Free will allows us to recognise His goodness and wisdom and choose to will His will. There are no examples in Scripture of someone not given the ability to choose, beginning with the archangel Lucifer. We understand that Satan was given the opportunity to choose. He was perfect in the day that God created him until iniquity was found in Him[226]. Jesus said that He did not remain in the truth, and He said that Satan was a liar and the father (or originator) of it[227]. If we let Scripture simply tell us about God and the events that have taken place, we come to an entirely different conclusion than when we force the meaning of each

---

[226] (Eze. 28)
[227] (Jn. 8:44)

scripture to comply with a preconceived theory about God and His works.

It was a terrible tragedy that the term grace became nearly defined as an opposite for free will in the controversy between Calvinism and Arminianism. Another tragedy is that the sovereignty of God was given a forced meaning of God's absolute control over every event. This theory was then forced on God and each individual that He had created and became the doctrine of unconditional determination of all souls either to Heaven or Hell. Such confusion ensued in the theological ideologies of men that Biblical words lost their meaning and were defined in such a way to support non-biblical concepts.

When we speak of grace, we should be referring to what God divinely does in His goodness on our behalf to redeem, keep, and develop us in all of His ways. When we speak of the sovereignty of God, it should be in terms of His holiness, His greatness and universal power. It should be a tribute to the One Who is infinitely wise and good, the One Who is infinitely righteous and thus can never do any wrong. The free will of man does not contradict the sovereignty of God, because God has sovereignly given us the right to voluntarily participate with His will. Unfortunately, men create a philosophical bias concerning the sovereignty of God and demand that every event in Scripture conform to their idea of that sovereignty. Thus, they insert their own ideas into everything that God is and has done, creating a God whose nature and image conforms to their own concepts.

For example, there is no place in Scripture that indicates that God designed or predetermined Adam and Eve to disobey Him. Yet because everything must be interpreted in view of their ideas of God's sovereignty (absolute control over every event), they make the argument that it had to be God's plan for Adam to fall. Once again, Calvin decided on an unconditional salvation or damnation for each individual before they were born, and he built his entire theology on that non-biblical premise. As Arminius argued, that makes God the Author of sin. It makes God an unjust Judge Who penalized and sentenced Adam and Eve to a punishment that was not out of their own will. However, once again, these are purely the philosophical ideas of men, not the plain report of Scripture. There is nowhere in Scripture that God indicates that He planned the demise of all mankind through the fall of Adam and Eve. There is nothing that would indicate that God is responsible for the sin of mankind, rather just the opposite! God has nothing whatsoever to do with sin and evil. He is absolutely pure and holy. When God saw the wickedness of men, He repented that He had made man[228]. Sin did not enter into the world because of the sovereign act of God's will or

---

[228] (Gen. 6:3)

predetermined plan – rather, sin entered into the world by one man's disobedience[229].

We believe in 'solo gratia' ("grace alone"), but this includes the response of men and their willingness to obey God. Men must be willing to respond to the call of God, and if they are, God's great salvation empowers them to obey. God alone acted on our part to do what we could never be worthy or deserving of. To say salvation is by God's grace alone, and thus men have no responsibility to respond to God, defies the many scriptures that prove otherwise. Jesus made the need for our response very clear when He said,

> "He that has My commandments and keeps them is the one who loves Me. And he who loves Me shall be loved by My Father, and I shall love him and reveal Myself to him." Judas (not Iscariot) said to Him, "Lord, what has happened that You are about to reveal Yourself to us and not to the world?" Jesus answered and said to him, "If anyone loves Me, he will keep My words, and My Father will love him, and We shall come to him and make Our dwelling place with him. Whoever does not love Me does not keep My words; and the word that you hear is not My own, but My Father's Who sent Me."
>
> (John 14:21-24)

---

[229] (Rom. 5:12-21)

There is no person with an honest heart toward God who would want to be disobedient to God. God, through Christ Jesus, restored the relationship that Adam's disobedience forfeited. Now, in this renewed relationship, we have the Spirit of the Son and a heart full of love for our heavenly Father. Through the sovereignty and goodness of God, we are saved by grace, but we must also recognize that God has required our free will to say, "Yes," to Him. Men must believe in order to be saved[230]. If men refuse to believe, they will be lost[231]. Human participation and responsibility is involved in salvation. God has willed that we recognize our sin, we repent and turn from our sin, and by turning to God, we place all of our trust in Christ Jesus.

To grasp what theologians and preachers preached before Augustine, we turn to those like Chrysostom, who was a 3rd century archbishop. Chrysostom was very clear on grace and free will:

> "He explicitly and ubiquitously undermines notions of a merely forensic righteousness in justification, and views faith as the human's catalyst for grace and all the faith-based virtues that come with it which constitute justifying righteousness. Furthermore, Chrysostom believes that faith, by bringing grace,

---
[230] (John 3:16; Acts 16:31)
[231] (John 3:35; Rom. 1:17-18)

enables the fulfillment of the written Law and the law of nature in the life of the believer."

(Cochran)

"John Chrysostom ... is without question the most dependable representative of the Christological and exegetical tradition of the 'School of Antioch.'"

(Bobrinskoy, 1984)

Repent and Believe

Grace has brought to us repentance unto life. Grace has brought to us a changed life and the ability to preach the message of change. The unchanging Christ Jesus, Who is the same yesterday, today, and forever, came and preached the Gospel of the Kingdom and commissioned us to do the same: to preach the exact same Gospel that He preached, not another gospel. The Gospel that He preached was:

> "Repent and believe."
> "Now after that John was put in prison, Jesus came into Galilee, preaching the Gospel of the Kingdom of God, and saying, 'The time is fulfilled, and the Kingdom of God is at hand. Repent, and believe the Gospel.'"
> (Mk. 1:14–15 cr Mt. 4:17)

Jesus told us that as the Father sent Him, He also sent us. He told us,

> "Go into all the world, and preach the Gospel to every creature. He who believes and is baptized shall be saved, but he who does not believe shall be damned."
>
> (Mk. 16:15–16)

When the Apostle Peter preached, he preached the same message,

> "Then Peter said to them, 'Repent, and be baptized, every one of you, in the name of Jesus Christ for the remission of sins, and you shall receive the gift of the Holy Ghost.'"
>
> (Ac. 2:38)

Again, when Peter and John were testifying of Jesus in Jerusalem, they said,

> "Repent therefore, and be converted, that your sins may be blotted out, when the times of refreshing shall come from the presence of the Lord."
>
> (Ac. 3:19)

When Simon had thought that he could purchase the ability to impart the Holy Spirit, Peter said,

> "...your heart is not right in the sight of God. Repent therefore of your wickedness, and pray to God, if perhaps the thought of your heart may be forgiven"
>
> (Acts 8:21–22).

Paul preached the same Gospel message saying that God commands all men everywhere to repent[232]. Paul testified to both the Greeks and the Jews:

> *"repentance toward God and faith towards the Lord Jesus Christ."*
>
> (Acts 20:21)

He preached that men must repent and turn to God and do works worthy of repentance[233].

There is no excuse to preach any other Gospel. This is the Gospel of grace –grace that has granted to all men the opportunity to repent and become a new creation. For men to think that grace is somehow magnified in their sin is unreasonable, they should have hearkened to Paul[234]. Grace is magnified in that we were delivered from sin and empowered to walk in obedience to God. Grace has beautified us with God's salvation. Grace has dressed us with the ornaments of His righteousness and holiness. Grace has called us to shine with the glory of the only begotten Son. Grace has made us one with Christ Jesus even as Christ Jesus is one with the Father, Grace has called us out of darkness into His marvelous light. No one should think that the darkness and shame of sin could

---

[232] (Acts 17:30)
[233] (Acts 26:20)
[234] (Rom. 6:1)

ever display any part of that which belongs to God, and grace belongs to God[235].

---

[235] (Jn 17:21-23)

Good Works Are Faith Works

> *"For by grace are you saved through faith; and that not of yourselves– it is the gift of God: not of works, lest any man should boast. For we are His workmanship, created in Christ Jesus unto good works, which God has foreordained that we should walk in them."*
>
> (Eph. 2:8-10)

The grace that saved us and made us a new creation also produces within our lives the works of the Holy Spirit. Paul goes on to complete the truth that he is communicating by describing the obedience that is the product of the gift of grace. He makes it very clear that God has ordained that we walk in the good works that we were created in Christ Jesus to have[236]. These works come forth out of the righteousness of God that we have been given: the righteousness of God which is by the faith of Jesus Christ– the very indwelling of God in our lives that works mightily within us.

The reality of walking in the ways of God as a new creation is communicated hundreds of times using words like works, deeds, obedience, faithfulness, etc. The Greek word 'ergon,' which is translated as "works" or "deeds," is

---

[236] (*e.g.* Eph. 2:10)

found 176 times in the Majority Text type. There is no mistaking the fact that it refers to walking in the ways of God. Of course, one of the classic mistakes that is made by many is that they fail to distinguish between the works of the Law and faith works, or what could also be classified as the works of the Spirit exemplified by the fruits of the Spirit.

Jesus said,

> "Let your light shine before men that they may see your good works and glorify your Father in Heaven."
>
> (Matt. 5:16)

Jesus Himself was mighty in works and word[237]. Jesus was sent to do the works of the Father[238]. The Father showed Jesus the works that He was to do[239]. Jesus classified the miracles that He did as works[240]. He said if He did not do the works of His Father that men should not believe Him[241]. He said it was the Father Who did the works through Him[242]. And the works were the proof that the Father was in Him[243]. Anyone who believes will do His works and greater works[244]. God called Barnabas and Paul unto the work of the ministry[245]. Paul preached that men

---

[237] (Lk. 24:19)
[238] (Jn. 5:30; 10:25, 37)
[239] (Jn. 5:19)
[240] (Jn. 5:36, 10:38, 14:11)
[241] (Jn. 10:37)
[242] (Jn. 14:10)
[243] (Jn. 10:38)
[244] (Jn. 14:12)
[245] (Acts 13:2)

should turn to God and do works of repentance[246]. God will reward men according to their works[247]. Those who are born again have the works of the Law written in their hearts[248]. Paul's ministry made the Gentiles obedient in word and works[249]. Men will receive rewards from God based on works[250]. We are to abound in the work of the Lord[251]. God enables us to abound in every good work[252].

There is a difference between Law works and faith works. We are to prove our works[253]. We are created in Christ Jesus unto good works[254]. We are to be fruitful in every good work[255]. All that we do in word and works we do in the name of Jesus[256]. God fulfills in us the work of faith and power[257]. God establishes us in every good word and work[258]. We are to be rich in good works[259]. We are prepared unto every good work by God[260]. We are to be a pattern of good works[261]. Jesus purified us and made us zealous for good works[262]. We are to be ready for every

---

[246] (Acts 26:20)
[247] (*e.g.* Matt. 16:27; Rom. 2:6)
[248] (Rom. 2:15)
[249] (Rom. 15:18)
[250] (*e.g.* Rom. 2:6; Rev. 22:12)
[251] (1 Cor. 15:58)
[252] (2 Cor. 9:8)
[253] (Gal. 6:4)
[254] (Eph. 2:10)
[255] (Col. 1:10)
[256] (Col. 3:17)
[257] (2 Thess. 1:11)
[258] (2 Thess. 2:17)
[259] (1 Tim. 6:18)
[260] (2 Tim. 2:21)
[261] (Tit. 2:7)
[262] (Tit. 2:14)

good work[263]. Those who have believed must be careful to maintain good works[264]. We are to provoke one another to love and good works[265]. God makes us perfect in every good work to do His will, working in us that which is well-pleasing in His sight[266]. Faith has works[267]. God will judge every man according to their works[268]. Men glorify God when they see our good works[269]. We are to love in actions and truth[270]. Jesus knows our works, and judgment is rendered accordingly[271].

We were children of wrath, and being already sentenced to death, there was no possibility of reprieve or buying our way out of that sentencing through good works. Only the immense expression of God's grace manifested through the death of Christ Jesus could pay our debt of sin. In the greatness of God's goodness, He manifested His love for us and gave us the two most precious things that He possessed: His only begotten Son to pay in full for our sins and to provide resurrection life and the gift of the Holy Spirit. Now, that which God's

---

[263] (2 Tim. 2:21, 3:17)
[264] (Tit. 3:8)
[265] (Heb. 10:24)
[266] (Heb. 13:21)
[267] (Jam. 2:14)
[268] (1 Pet. 1:17)
[269] (1 Pet. 2:12)
[270] (1 Jn. 3:18)
[271] (Mt. 5:16; Luke 24:19; John 4:34, 5:20, 36, 9:3-4, 10:25, 37-38, 14:10-12; Acts 13:2, 26:20; Romans 2:6, 15, 15:18; 1 Cor. 3:13-15, 15:58; 2 Cor. 9:8; Gal. 2:16, 3:5, 6:4; Eph. 2:10; Col. 1:10, 3:17; 1 Thess. 1:3; 2 Thess. 1:11, 2:17; 1 Tim. 2:10, 5:10, 25, 6:18; 2 Tim. 2:21, 3:17; Titus 2:7,14, 3:1, 8,14; Hebrews 10:24, 13:21; James 1:25, 2:14, 17, 18, 20, 22, 26; 1 Peter 1:17, 2:12; 1 John 3:18; Rev. 2:2, 5, 6, 9, 13, 19, 22-23, 26, 3:1, 2, 8, 15)

grace purchased and provided for us is how we live. The new creation does by nature those things that are contained in the Law of God. These are not works of human ability, but the works of the life of Christ Jesus that now dwells within us – the works of the Holy Spirit that spring up and flow out in an unlimited expression of the life of God as we yield ourselves to Him. The grace by which we are saved provided

> *"all things that pertain to life and godliness."*
> (2 Peter 1:3)

God gave us everything that we need according to His divine power to do all that He has required of us.

> "God Himself gives the grace to make His servant pure, and 'With the pure Thou dost show Thyself pure.'"
> (James E. Rosscup, 2008)

The Same Grace that Saved Us Matures Us

One of the most important things to grasp is that even those defined as "little ones," and even "infants," in Christ have their sins forgiven for His name sake[272]. Growing in grace is maturing in grace by the work of grace[273]. When we were born again, we were born of God. Our spirits were joined to the Holy Spirit. Our lives became united together with the life of Jesus. We were given His righteousness, which is the righteousness of God. We were given His holiness, which is the holiness of God.

We were given His life instantaneously, and we were given His righteousness and holiness when we were given His life. However, as newborn babies, we must grow and develop. We grow and develop in His righteousness and holiness by walking with Him and responding to His instructions. Much like we grow and develop in all the human attributes from birth until we die, so we grow up into all that has been given to us. We do not slowly obtain His righteousness and holiness through some develop-

---
[272] (1 John 2:12-13)
[273] (2 Peter 3:18)

mental process any more than we would obtain his life. His life becomes our possession the moment we are born again, because we are in Him and He is in us. We are not obtaining either the righteousness of God or His holiness any more than we are obtaining grace or salvation – it has been freely given. If we were in a process of being born again, then we might say that we are being made holy or righteous, but that is not the case – we have been born again and possess His divine nature.

There is nothing that God has that can be earned or acquired on the basis of our own works. God has freely given us all things. Now we must be willing to grow up into Him in all that He has freely given[274]. We were born into the family of God with a new nature in similar ways that Christ Jesus was born into this world. He then grew up into all that God had purposed for Him to be[275]. Growth brings an increased manifestation of all that we are. Even so, we grow up into Him to be all that God has purposed us to be.

We have been given the righteousness of God, but when we are born again, we do not fully express His righteousness in our behavior. We were given His holiness, but we do not fully express His holiness in our conduct. As we yield ourselves to the Holy Spirit, His righteousness and holiness that we possess are revealed

---
[274] (Eph. 4:15)
[275] (Luke 2:52)

through our lives. Maturity develops us into the full expression of His righteousness and holiness. To say that we have His righteousness and holiness only in a theologically positional way and without an out-working in our lives is most definitely contrary to the Scripture. We were made holy to be holy just as He is holy. We were made righteous to be righteous just as He is righteousness[276]. God is at work in us and He is the One Who perfects (matures and finishes) everything that He has made us to be.

So exactly what is Peter saying when He says "grow in grace" (2 Peter 3:18)? We conclude that He is referring to the ongoing work of His grace in our lives. Therefore growing in grace is growing up into Christ Jesus, increasing in the knowledge of God, and increasing with the increase of God[277]. Just as in the natural life everything grows up into its full potential, even so do we in our spiritual life. The seed of the redwood certainly looks nothing like the redwood, but everything is contained in the redwood seed so that it will become one of the tallest trees that exists. When we were born again, we were created in Christ Jesus unto good works. However, like the redwood seed, our infancy only develops into all that has been given us as we, as newborn babies, grow through the nourishment of the Word of God[278].

---

[276] (Romans 14:17; Ephesians 5:9; 1 Peter 2:24; 1 John 3:7)
[277] (Eph. 4:15; Col. 1:10, 2:19)
[278] (1 Pet. 2:2, 1:23)

Grace: The Door has been open to All

Everything that we are in Christ Jesus is a result of God's grace. First we are given the grace that has created us in Christ Jesus and supplied us with all that belongs to the divine nature[279]. Beyond that, God gives special divine abilities out of the grace that is given for special works. Therefore we have gifts differing from one another based on the grace that is given[280]. God does not place a limit on how many gifts or special divine abilities that we can function in. Still, the Holy Spirit divides individually to each person according to His will[281]. Therefore, we can understand that grace can also develop and flourish into many divine abilities in our lives. Although we may only operate in a measure, we have been given all of God's fullness[282]. That fullness becomes expressed as we come to know the love of Christ that passes knowledge through the power of the Holy Spirit Who works within us[283]. The fullness manifests as we respond to the measureless supply of the Holy Spirit's baptism upon our lives. The fulness is witnessed as His life and power flow out of us like rivers[284].

---

[279] (2 Peter 1:4)
[280] (Rom. 12:6)
[281] (1 Cor. 12:11)
[282] (John 1:16)
[283] (Eph. 3:18-20)
[284] (John 7:37-39)

The Grace that Purchased Us Preserves Us

We are kept by the power of God[285]. What a great definition of the grace of God that keeps us! Grace is what only God can do for us. What He is doing is keeping us by His power. There is no power that can pluck us out of His hand[286]. We have been given great assurance that God is our Keeper, our Protector, and the One Who continually watches over us. However, to think that there needs to be no participation together with Him is a horrific mistake. The Lord has given us His strength, His power, and His might to stand against every power of darkness that would attempt to draw us away[287].

The prayer is that our whole spirit, soul, and body be preserved blameless[288]. The purpose of Christ Jesus is to present us holy, unblameable, and unreproveable in His sight. He has given us this kind of purity because He presents us now and in the future in the body of His

---

[285] (1 Peter 1:5, Jude 24)
[286] (John 10:28)
[287] (Eph. 6:10-12)
[288] (1 Thess. 5:23)

flesh[289]. He is the One Who is able to keep us from stumbling and to present us faultless before His presence[290]. He has made us holy and without blemish[291]. It is by and through His blood alone that we find ourselves dressed in the righteousness of the saints[292]. We can be certain that the One Who began a good work in us will finish it[293]. All we must do is trust Him and yield ourselves to His work of grace[294]. When God reigns in our life, who or what can overthrow Him or anyone who is in Him?

Satan has no authority to take from us what only God could give to us. We are not left to our own strength to deal with such a great adversary. God has destroyed him who has the power of death[295]. Jesus said to the Father, "Keep through Your own name those who You gave to Me," so that we may remain one with the Father just as Jesus is One with the Father (John 17:11). What power could ever overthrow the power of the Father? There is none! Christ Jesus is able to save us to the utmost because He makes intercession for the saints[296].

There are those who want to continue in sin and live a life contrary to the ways of God and yet desire to claim

---

[289] (Col. 1:22, Heb. 10:20)
[290] (Jude 1:24)
[291] (Eph. 5:27)
[292] (Rev. 19:8; 1 Cor. 1:30)
[293] (Phm. 1:6)
[294] (Rom. 6:16-22, 8:14)
[295] (Heb. 2:14, 2 Tim. 1:10, John 12:31)
[296] (Heb. 7:25)

these promises. However, nothing could be further from the truth. Those who would go on in sin, believing that sin is somehow acceptable to God after receiving the knowledge of the truth, will find that there is nothing but a fiery indignation awaiting them[297]. We should not trample underfoot the blood of Jesus that cleansed us and made us holy and outrage the Spirit of grace[298]. Even as Israel continually refused to obey God – and chose rather to walk in their iniquity and were judged – so we also will be judged if we refuse to obey[299].

> "The Apostle Paul insisted, as strongly as anyone could, on the doctrines of grace, shewing that all was ordered by God according to the counsel of his own will: yet no Apostle spoke more strongly than he on the danger of apostasy; or taught more forcibly the necessity of continual watchfulness on our part…"
>
> (Charles Simeon, 1833).

We have been given the best help, the greatest intercessor, and the keeping power of God. He has given us the divine nature, His divine power, the Shepherd and Bishop of our soul, and His unfailing love. Yet, there is a choice that each person makes. Any person can choose not to walk with God and refuse His help and

---

[297] (Heb. 10:26-27)
[298] (Heb. 10:29)
[299] (Heb. 10:30, Deut. 32:35-36, Ps. 135:14)

protection[300]. There are many who say they know the Lord, but God says that He never knew them because they never stopped with their iniquity and never participated with His will[301].

All we need to do is simply say, "yes," to God and His will. There will be no power that will ever be able to hinder what God is committed to doing for you, in you, and with you.

> "Abstain from every form of evil, and the God of peace Himself makes you holy in every way and complete. And may your entire spirit, and soul, and body be preserved blameless unto the coming of our Lord Jesus Christ."
>
> (1 Thess. 5:22-23)

All we need to do is to continue in grace[302]. Do not allow the doctrines of men to cause you to be removed from the grace of Christ[303]. Properly respond to the Spirit of Grace – the grace that has brought salvation teaches us to deny ungodliness and worldly lusts and instead live righteously[304]. Recognize that we must be diligent with all the things that the grace of God has provided for unless we fall short of the grace of God[305]. We must hold fast to

---
[300] (1 Cor. 6:9-10, Eph. 5:6, 1 John 3:7-8, Gal. 5:21)
[301] (Mt. 7:21, 1 John 2:17)
[302] (Acts 13:43)
[303] (Gal. 1:6, 5:4)
[304] (Ti. 2:12; Heb. 10:29)
[305] (Hebrews 12:15)

our confession of faith without wavering, for He is faithful Who promised[306].

---

[306] (Heb. 10:23)

The Throne of Grace

"We should come with boldness to the throne of grace, that we may receive mercy and may find grace to help in time of need."

(Heb. 4:16)

Grace did not begin with the coming of Jesus, for God's grace is a part of Who He is, and has been shown and given to man from the beginning. God is the God of all grace and has always been so[307]. However, the fullest expression of grace came to us by Jesus[308]. The God of all grace has called the whole of mankind into His eternal glory.

"And the God of all grace, Who called you into His eternal glory inChrist Jesus, after you have suffered a little, will restore you, establish, strengthen, set firm."

(1 Pet. 5:10)

The love and mercy of God have provided us with access to the throne of grace where we can obtain mercy and also find help with everything that we have to deal

---
[307] (1 Peter 5:10; Mal. 3:6; James 1:17; Ps. 102:27; Ex. 34:6)
[308] (John 1:17; Rom. 5:21, 6:14)

with as we are opposed by every trial and every form of temptation and sin. The mercy seat was provided for the people of Israel during the Old Covenant, but now God has provided all who will come to Him with greater access to His help. Whereas the priest approached the mercy seat with great fear and trepidation because of the lethal potency of sin, we can come boldly to the throne of grace because of the blood of Jesus that has cleansed us and made us holy[309]. God in His mercy offers forgiveness and help with every trouble that we find ourselves in. God will not withhold His mercy from anyone who comes to Him by His Son Jesus. When a person calls upon the name of the Lord Jesus, God is there to rescue. He will help everyone who comes to Him by Christ Jesus. We can draw near to Him in full assurance of the faith, having had the blood of Jesus applied to our hearts[310].

Job complained that he could not find how to approach God:

> "Oh that I knew where I might find Him! That I might come to His seat!"
>
> (Job 23:3)

This is not the case for us. Whatever we are dealing with, we are told exactly what to do and where to come: "Come to the throne of grace." We are given great assurance that

---

[309] (Heb. 10:10, 14, 29, 13:12)
[310] (Heb. 10:22)

God will intervene on our behalf. God has highly exalted His Son and given Him a name above every name. He is seated at the right hand of the Father, and there He serves as the One Who intercedes for us. The efficacy of His blood to remove every sin and the faithfulness of His love to strengthen and secure us are guaranteed. If we sin, if we are hurting, if we are uncertain, or are overwhelmed by trials and temptations, God is calling us to come and receive the mercy and help that only He can give. One of the great defining expressions of grace is that we have free and unlimited access to God. Additionally, we not only have free access to Him at any time, but His love and mercy are there to supply all that we need.

When we come to the throne of grace, we are met by our high priest, Christ Jesus. He officiates with His blood to cleanse every sin of those who come to Him. During the Old Covenant, the high priest carried the blood within the veil to apply it to the mercy seat, which was also a throne of God. Yet, Christ Jesus cleanses our sins with His own blood before the throne of grace when we come to Him. The One Who ever lives to make intercession for us is able to save us to the utmost.

> "Be it so, our sins have been most heinous: yet are we assured, that 'his blood will cleanse from all sin,' and that they who are washed in it, shall be as wool, and their crimson sins be white as snow."
>
> (Charles Simeon, 1833)

Grace: The Door has been open to All

"'And may find grace to help in time of need.' He said well, 'for help in time of need.' If you approach now, he means, you will receive both grace and mercy, for you approach 'in time of need.' … Now he sits granting pardon, but when the end is come, then he rises up to judgment" -Chrysostom

(Erik M. Heen and Philip D. W. Krey, 2005).

It is the blood of Jesus that cleanses us from all sin.

"If we walk in the light as He is in the light, we have fellowship with one another, and the blood of Jesus Christ His Son cleanses us from all sin."

(1 John 1:7)

The goodness of God has made an immense provision for us of complete cleansing from our sin and a provision for any time in the future "if" we sin. The blood not only forgives but also cleanses us. The case of "cleansing" is in the present tense, but it certainly is also there for the future.

"καθαρίζει is the present tense, and must be kept to its present meaning."

(Henry Alford, 1976)

However, we would be careless if we did not view this scripture in light of those who say that they have fellowship with God, are saved and washed in the blood, but walk in darkness[311].Such people are liars, are not in the truth, and cannot lay claim to the immense mercy of the blood that cleanses. There is always the opportunity for them to repent, turn to God, and be met with His mercy, but there must be truth.

We have been washed in the blood, cleansed, and made holy when we first gave our lives to Jesus. We were purchased and made holy and righteous by His blood, having been washed from all our sins in His own blood[312]. We were redeemed from all iniquity and purified[313]. Yet, if there is any cleansing needed for now or the future, God has abundantly supplied. The provision of cleansing is for those who walk in the light: those who are walking in truth. Those walking in truth have the testimony of the Spirit and the fellowship of love one for another[314]. There is great provision for all those who walk in truth. Any sin that is committed and confessed is also cleansed by our great High Priest at the throne of grace[315]. (Of course for those like the Anglican theologian Alford who believe that those once born again still possess the sin nature, they view verse 7 as an ongoing purifying work that takes place day-by-day until complete sanctification occurs – His blood being the purifying medium, whereby we gradually,

---

[311] (1 John 1:6)
[312] (Acts 20:28; 1 Cor. 6:11; Rev. 1:5)
[313] (Titus 2:14)
[314] (1 John 2:9-10, 3:4)
[315] (1 John 1:9; Heb. 4:16)

being already justified, become pure and clean from all sin. And this application of Christ's blood is made by the Spirit Who dwells in us. (Henry Alford, 1976).) So much of Scripture has been interpreted in view of Christians still possessing a sin nature which effectively communicates the concept of being cleansed, but not really cleansed; of being born again, but not really a new creation; of possessing the divine nature, but still partly bound by the power of sin.

Still, the Scripture declares the immeasurable grace of God: that we have been born of God; that we are a new creation and all the old things have passed away; that everything has become new and everything about our lives is of God; that we are washed with the water of regeneration and renewing of the Holy Spirit; that we are in the Spirit and no longer in an unregenerate state (flesh); that we are renewed in righteousness and true holiness; that we possess the divine nature; that we have been made one with Christ Jesus; that we are the temple of the Holy Spirit and that God dwells in us; that the Holy Spirit is with us and in us; that the life of God, the life of the Holy Spirit, flows forth from us like rivers; that the old has been put to death; that the nature of sin has been destroyed; that the body of sins have been removed, cut away by the circumcision of the heart; that our inward man, the hidden man of our heart has been raised up together with Christ Jesus; that God dwells in us and walks in us; that we have a new heart; that we have a new spirit; that our spirit has been joined unto the Holy Spirit; that we have purified our souls by obeying the truth; that our spirit, soul, and body are preserved blameless; that we can present our bodies holy and acceptable to God; that we are as He is in this world; that we are not of this world just as He is not of this world; that we are righteous even as He is righteous; that we walk just He walks; that we have His fullness; that we are filled with all of His fullness; that the ways of God are written on our hearts and minds; that all things that pertain to His life and godliness have been given to us; that we are strong in the Lord and the power of His might; that sin has no dominion over us; that we are the servants of righteousness; that we are translated out of the kingdom of darkness into the Kingdom of the dear Son; that we are seated together with Him in a heavenly realm; that no power of Satan can harm us; that we have authority over all of the powers of darkness; that we are made holy; that we are the light of the world; that we stand in Christ's stead in this age; that we are a new man; that He has given us His glory.

What God Has Willed

The Lord tells us to be perfect just as He is perfect; to be holy just as He is Holy; to be strong in His strength; to love just like He loves. We are to imitate God. We are to walk just like He walks. We are to imitate Jesus. We are to be pure just as He is pure; to be righteous just as He is righteous. He made us one with Himself. He made us the light of the world. We are to have His faith. We are to be filled with the Holy Spirit. We are to live in the Spirit. We are to walk in the Spirit. We are to do the will of the Father. We are told that nothing shall be impossible for us. We are called to come and learn of Him; to take up His servitude. We are to grow up into Him in all things. We are told to follow in His footsteps. We are to be conformed to the image of the Son. We are not to be conformed to this world. We are to be perfect in Christ Jesus. We are to be godly. We are not of this world just as He is not of this world. He has raised us up together with His Son.

God has made us all of these things and more. He is the One Who is perfecting everything that concerns us. He is the One Who teaches us and guides us. He is the One Who both wills and does of His good pleasure in our lives as we yield to Him. He is the One Who mentors us and provides all that we need according to His riches in glory. He corrects us, chastens us, and develops us in all of His ways. His vision for us is to live the life that He lives; to mature into the fullness of the ministry of Jesus; to be the precious fruit of the Earth. He wants us to seek first the Kingdom of God and His righteousness. He wants us to hunger and thirst after righteousness. He has made us His temple where He now dwells. He wants to walk in us. He desires to reveal His Son in us. He wants us to rule and reign with Him. He wants His gifts of the Spirit to be demonstrated in our lives. He desires to be glorified in us and us to be glorified in Him. He wants us to ask what we will and He will do it for us.

He is our Savior, our Healer, our Deliverer, our way-Maker, our Provider, our Protector, and our Perfecter. He is our Redeemer, our Life, our Expectation, and our Hope. He is the One Who is with us and will never leave us. He guides us with His eyes. He keeps us with His power. He surrounds us with His love and upholds us with His strength. All of His delights are with us and He has set His affections upon us. There is no power that can prevail against us, for He is on our side. He is our Father, Christ Jesus our brother, and the Holy Spirit our constant companion.

He is all of these things to us and more! He has given everything that He has for us so that we may have everything that pertains to His life and godliness. He has worked by His divine power and is working by His divine power so that we can be all that He created us to be. Our God wants there to be no sin in our life. He wants there to be no trace of the demonic power and the darkness that once ruled our life. In His grace and by His grace He brings all these things to pass as we yield ourselves to Him in complete surrender to His will.

References

Gerald Bray, ed., Romans (Revised), Ancient Christian Commentary on Scripture (Downers Grove, IL: InterVarsity Press, 1998), 276.

James E. Rosscup, An Exposition on Prayer in the Bible: Igniting the Fuel to Flame Our Communication with God (Bellingham, WA: Lexham Press, 2008), 524.

Alexander MacLaren, Expositions of Holy Scripture: 2 Corinthians 7–12, Galatians, Philippians 1–3 (Bellingham, WA: Logos Bible Software, 2009), 44.

Grant R. Osborne, John: Verse by Verse, ed. Jeffrey Reimer et al., Osborne New Testament Commentaries (Bellingham, WA: Lexham Press, 2018), 35.

John Chrysostom, "Homilies of St. John Chrysostom, Archbishop of Constantinople, on the Gospel of St. John," in Saint Chrysostom: Homilies on the Gospel of St. John and Epistle to the Hebrews, ed. Philip Schaff, trans. G. T. Stupart, vol. 14, A Select Library of the Nicene and Post-

Nicene Fathers of the Christian Church, First Series (New York: Christian Literature Company, 1889), 49.

David A. Case and David W. Holdren, 1-2 Peter, 1-3 John, Jude: A Commentary for Bible Students (Indianapolis, IN: Wesleyan Publishing House, 2006), 288.

H. D. M. Spence-Jones, ed., The Pulpit Commentary: Romans, The Pulpit Commentary (London; New York: Funk & Wagnalls Company, 1909), 120.

Robert Jamieson, A. R. Fausset, and David Brown, Commentary Critical and Explanatory on the Whole Bible, vol. 2 (Oak Harbor, WA: Logos Research Systems, Inc., 1997), 331.

Finis Jennings Dake, The Dake Annotated Reference Bible (Dake Publishing, 1997), Col 2:9.

Arno C. Gaebelein, The Annotated Bible: Philippians to Hebrews, vol. 8 (Bellingham, WA: Logos Bible Software, 2009), 67.

Gerhard Kittel, Geoffrey W. Bromiley, and Gerhard Friedrich, Theological Dictionary of the New Testament (Grand Rapids, MI: Eerdmans, 1964–), 49.

Charles Simeon, Horae Homileticae: James to Jude, vol. 20 (London: Holdsworth and Ball, 1833), 369.

Charles Simeon, Horae Homileticae: 2 Timothy to Hebrews, vol. 19 (London: Holdsworth and Ball, 1833), 343.

William R. Baker and Paul K. Carrier, James-Jude: Unlocking the Scriptures for You, Standard Bible Studies (Cincinnati, OH: Standard, 1990), 242.

Mark Galli and Ted Olsen, "Introduction," 131 Christians Everyone Should Know (Nashville, TN: Broadman & Holman Publishers, 2000), 41–42.

McClintock and Strong Biblical Cyclopedia Online
Erik M. Heen and Philip D. W. Krey, eds., Hebrews, Ancient Christian Commentary on Scripture (Downers Grove, IL: InterVarsity Press, 2005), 69.

Matthew Poole, Annotations upon the Holy Bible, vol. 3 (New York: Robert Carter and Brothers, 1853), 930.

Henry Alford, Alford's Greek Testament: An Exegetical and Critical Commentary, vol. 4 (Grand Rapids, MI: Guardian Press, 1976), 428.

Henry Alford, *Alford's Greek Testament: An Exegetical and Critical Commentary*, vol. 4 (Grand Rapids, MI: Guardian Press, 1976), 428.

About the Author

Dr. Mark Spitsbergen is the Senior Pastor of the Abiding Place in San Diego, California where he and his wife Anne have pastored since 1985. He holds a Bachelor of Arts Degree (BA) in Biology/Chemistry from Point Loma Nazarene University, a Master of Science (MS) from the University of Saint Andrews, a Doctorate of Theology (ThD) from School of Bible Theology, as well as a Doctorate of Ministry (D. Min.) from Life Christian University. He has been studying Biblical languages since 1983. He began his study of biblical languages at PLNU and also studied at UCSD with Dr. David Noel Freedman.

www.ingramcontent.com/pod-product-compliance
Lightning Source LLC
LaVergne TN
LVHW041337080426
835512LV00006B/509